Paid with
Plastic

The Art of the Steal

Will Black

Published by JETLAUNCH

Copyright © 2024 Will Black

ISBN: 979-8-89079-183-2 (hardcover)
ISBN: 979-8-89079-184-9 (paperback)
ISBN: 979-8-89079-185-6 (ebook)

TABLE OF CONTENTS

III. HOW MUCH IS TAKEN OUT?

IV. IT'S THE END

"The first step in avoiding a trap is knowing of its existence."

–Thufir Hawat,
Master of Assassins
Dune

PREFACE

One could use so many analogies here, like Thufir Hawat's training from the book *Dune,* for example. He's the chief strategist for House Atreides. He's a human computer, but as Master of Assassins, he knows every trick in the book and thus works to keep House Atreides *alive*—that is to say, keep assassins out. He knows how because he knows how he would get them in if he wanted.

Or Carey Grant in *To Catch a Thief.* Who doesn't like a vintage movie? A thief to catch a thief. Well played, Hitchcock. Grant's character is a jewel thief—the best of the best. He's retired, but someone is robbing jewels—in his style, no less. It takes a master to catch that.

Those are exciting versions. A very boring version is Accounting 101. This is where one injects espresso into your retinas—dry, boring. They teach you the numbers and the basic setup. Then, they teach you to steal. No kidding. The first quarter of that class is theft. Here's how it's done. Here's every major way to steal that I've seen as a teacher who also does accounting and forensic accounting on the side, and a couple of others to boot. No, forensic accounting doesn't involve Quincy or any other morgue. A forensic accountant is someone who comes in and looks for a thief when something has gone down.

They teach you to steal so you can catch it. Here, I will show you numerous ways people rob others blind via their businesses and how they take plastic as payment. Some people may think this is like an anarchist's cookbook and adopt this. Shame. Your momma didn't raise you like that. Nobody dreams of stealing as a kid. Go back to that. It'll make your grandmother smile.

For those of you who want to know how to avoid the trap like Thufir teaches, your training begins now. Pay attention. The assassins are at the door.

If you need help with anything here, or would just like someone to do the math for you, go to https://qr.link/dMiltp or click the QR code and we'll take it from there.

I

THE NECESSARY
EVIL

Okay, let's admit one thing—arcades knew what they were doing.

You go in, exchange your cash for tokens, and play. You had to buy the tokens because that's all the machines took. Best of all, you had to use all your tokens for the arcade. You play by the rules, or you don't play at all. It's the very definition of a pay-to-play scenario.

What if I told you to shake the scales from your eyes? That the world has become the arcade, and the token is now a small rectangle of plastic? The difference is that the onus is put on the seller. Do you want to get in the game? For clients to come in your door? You need to accept plastic.

My grandmother, a businesswoman in her own right, said you fight for too long and hard to get every customer in your door, so you'd better not turn one away. What business these days can actually afford to be cash only? Checks? Would you like fries with your order of fraud?

To get a business to fly, whether you have investors or you've bootstrapped so hard that your eyes barely look over the boot itself, every customer is precious. They have choices. Lots and lots of choices. You will fight hard enough just to be one of those choices so you won't let them leave because you didn't take their primary form of payment. If you're selling online, plastic is water in the desert; it's the only thing you want.

The system knows that. It's pumping cards out so hard and fast that you'd never believe it. Every college student has pre-approved cards shooting into their mailboxes faster than they can open the letters. Is it dangerous? Is it unethical? Why would they care? They'll earn interest in the cards from the students who have poor decision-making skills (facts are facts, don't get mad at me), and they'll get a percentage from the businesses that have to accept the plastic to survive. It's Jell-O all over again.

1

WATCH IT WIGGLE

Jell-O has a fascinating history.

First, there were aspics. If you don't know what aspic is, think of savory Jell-O made out of boiling bones and serving it embedded with meats, fish, pureed veggies, and other things. If you could take your great-grandmother's moth-ball-ridden attic, press it in a mold and make it jiggle, then eat it—you'd have an aspic. Look it up if you think this is too amazingly delicious to be true. Oddly, It can be very healthy.

Even on ships, they had what was called "portable soup," which was soup cooked down until it was gelatinous, making it easy to store and use for convalescing patients. The inventor Peter Cooper took the idea and made gelatin as a powder that could later be activated with hot water. He just couldn't do anything with it and wanted to focus on glue. Yes, glue.

In steps Pearl and May. The Waits couple got the patent and decided it was a good idea, but it was as dull as watching Grandpa snore. They added fruit syrups for flavor and dubbed it Jell-O. It tasted great, but they just couldn't do anything with it at the end of the day. Then along came Frank Woodward, who bought the idea for $450.

Frank knew what to do. He had recipes designed solely around Jell-O, printed them in a small booklet, and put them on the doorsteps and in the mailboxes of homes all around the area. Then, he beat it to the local grocer and told him he had better buy a whole lot of Woodward's Jell-O because people were about to come rolling in. Woodward wasn't wrong, and the idea worked. Grocers were inundated with demand and questions about this new product. They bought all Woodward would sell them, and the first viral marketing campaign was in the books.

Your business is now the local grocer, and you better have what the customer has been preprogrammed with (and it's not Jell-O). It's the ability to take plastic.

The problem is that most people barely understand how their credit cards work. Almost no one understands how their business's merchant account works. In case you are brand new to this game, a merchant account is how a business takes debit and credit cards as payment. Clients come in, pick their items, swipe their cards, and twenty-four to forty-eight hours later, the money goes into the business checking account.

Let's say you're opening your business, go to a bank (usually the one where you have your personal checking account), hand them your business license and Federal Tax ID number, and tell them you need a business checking account and the ability to accept credit cards and debit cards from customers. I have to state it like that because sometimes one doesn't know till they know, and this gets asked daily in banks across the country.

The banker working with you opens your business checking account, and then they set up your merchant account. They're not just putting a credit card terminal on your business counter; they're also putting a hand in your pocket.

This is the most important thing I can tell anyone. Let those who have ears listen. Everyone up the food chain makes money on your business whenever your customer swipes a card. Every time. They are allowed to profit from you and your work. If not, they wouldn't have built the system. They can make a reasonable profit, but wholesale smoke and mirrors induce a feeling of helplessness and ignorance so that business owners quit trying to follow up, which is less than kosher. But it's done every day for the sole reason of keeping you quiet, compliant, and, most importantly, from using your ability to move around in a free market.

II

STATEMENTS: IF IT CAN'T BE READ, IT CAN'T BE USED

You'll hear me often say, "*Use makes mastery*." Truer words, my friend, were rarely spoken. The converse is also true. If you can't use it, you'll feel like an amateur.

If you're an adult of almost any age, you have a statement of some kind—some form that lists everything you either used, consumed, or were billed for. Electric bill statements, phone bills, but probably the best comparison is a simple, straightforward checking statement. These show all the checks you wrote, things billed to your debit card, and, of course, the fees. Lots of fees.

Not dissimilar is your merchant statement, which shows all the sales you made at your business that were paid for via your merchant account in the form of credit cards, debit cards, and rewards cards, which come every month. It shows the cards, their types (very important), and how you were billed for each one. The only problem is no one can read it. Really. Not even professionals.

Right now, readers are thinking that is a pretty hefty claim, so I'll give you an example for clarity. My industry has a business paper that's often read called *The Green Sheet*. I'll let the individual guess the color of the periodical. It's distinctive. I do not encourage people to read it. Like most industry pieces, it's a bit dry unless you're well-heeled in the system. A spontaneous coma may have occurred for all I know, while those well-versed in merchant account taxonomy only get a stinging headache.

Just the same, we read it. We use it. I have to say, though, that a few years back, one story knocked my fillings loose. It was written by a senior VP in the industry who had been in from the beginning. He was wealthy and knew everything there was to know in our world of businesses and plastic, and his sole job at his company was to write his company's merchant statement. In other words, he designed the statement that thousands of clients who used his group would attempt to read every month to see what they were being charged at their place of business. And he spoke the bold, naked truth when he stated, "I can't read my competition's statements."

That should give you hope and break your heart at the same time. He *designs* statements and can't read the one from another company? Hell no, he can't. They are not supposed to be read. As I have written in business periodicals, merchant blogs, and every training course and college class I have ever spoken to, statements are made to have as much data and as little information as possible.

Drink that in.

Control of the information means control of the business. Control of you. Control of the money. These pieces are quite simply designed to intimidate so badly that the average person out-and-out lies to themselves, thinking, *I'll sit down and read it later* as they put it in a drawer. They move on; the business has other needs. There are some people at some businesses who actually open them, look for certain numbers, and transfer that information to a spreadsheet. In truth, though, that's not reading. That's transcribing a few numbers, then putting the fairly useless document away.

You see, it can be deciphered if you really know what you're doing. The senior VP of the company who designs his company's statement can break down the competition's statements. He can take a calculator and reverse engineer its core pieces to get what he needs. He just can't pick it up and read it like a water bill. Most people can't do that. Your average dentist, mechanic, bar owner, and hair stylist, while gifted in their individual fields, generally can't do it. You need specialists. You need a third party who can break down what you can't. We're going to crack open the gearbox and take a broad-stroke look at deciphering further, but first, why is that a big need?

1

LET ME TELL YOU ABOUT THE INSURANCE AGENTS I HAVE FIRED

Many of you will be better at this than I am, and you're not even insurance agents. Insurance isn't my thing. I'm okay with that. I also have a fantastic memory. Seriously. I have glanced at things and remembered them. But I have a friend, and I cannot remember her street address. I just can't lock it in. I have tried mnemonic devices and shear route-force will. I can't do it. I don't know why, but I am both okay with it and confounded because I am normally good at it.

Insurance is like that for me. I get it as a whole—pay a small amount now and hedge my bet against a need for a huge expense later. Fine, but that's it. I refuse to try to decipher the system. I hire people for that. That's their job. (A couple of insurance professionals out there just yelled, "Amen!") They're specialists. You get a specialist on your team who you can trust, breaks down what they do every day in simple terms, and lets you get back to what you do, and *you've struck gold*. Get a few of those in various streams of your life besides just insurance, and you are now a rocket ship.

I have fired insurance agents, though. Not for ignorance, they knew their stuff. Not for timeliness, as they showed up when called. Please pay attention to this next thing, as I think the world is sorely lacking here, and the professional who avoids this mistake will line their pockets and secure their future. They refused to avoid useless jargon and would just vomit it out—not just a little either, but quickly and in long paragraphs of industry-only terms in quick succession. They refused to avoid it. One all but refused to use anything but worthless industry jargon.

I would stop them—politely, mind you—and ask that they speak to me in everyday terms. "Garble, garble, garble," would be the refrain. I'd stop them again, slightly more firmly, and suggest basic terminology. They'd giggle like I'd just suggested they were inbred, and like a good salesman, they would laugh it off. "Well, you see, you have an eighty-sixty-forty, two-thirds agrarian cycle plan, and because of the renoberation of the deficit…"

Full stop. I'd explain for the third time.

"Joe [not his name], seriously. I am not in insurance. I do not understand eight of the nine terms you are using. Please stop. Just use common terms—common, like an eighth grader. Literally, talk down to me. If you don't, I will have to fire you and get another agent who will."

Understand that I have a stomach full of acid even saying that. I don't want that kind of confrontation, but the person who was making money from my account might as well have been speaking in Sanskrit—and on purpose, especially since I had laid out the arrangement for the conversation two times. That's called being a good customer. If one of my clients said, "Please just tell me like this…" I'd have long since done so. In fact, clients at the beginning of my career asked me to lay things out in simple terms, so I have endeavored to do as they asked. The client who tells you what they want *buys* when you give it to them.

What did I get after laying down the law? "Garble, garble, garble renoberation of the fiscal economy, garble, garble." There is now a level of distrust. Either he has profound disrespect for me or is stealing outright and can't show me something simple as it would show overpayment.

I stood up, thanked him for his time, told him that, unfortunately, I couldn't use him in the future, left the conference room, and walked to my office. I was done. My business partner who handled the insurance came in a few minutes later, and I frankly stated that he was to find another insurance agent and pre-warn them of these events. Also, he was to make sure Joe understood he had been terminated and why.

2

THE OLD YARD ART BIKE GUY

The next insurance agent did the same. I can't make this up.

I stopped her and recounted all these previous interactions. I told her that if I understood insurance the way she did, *I wouldn't need her.* I'd just do it myself. I told her that I fired the last guy. I didn't want to, but he refused to service my account, and by that, I meant taking time to explain.

It got through. She composed herself and moved forward when she realized I would fire her for useless jargon and that I actually encouraged her to talk to me like a child as far as this was concerned. I am a smart man. I don't find it offensive because it's not what I do.

When I started the restoration of a 1964 BSA motorcycle from Britain that was fifty years old and had been all but yard art for at least a decade, I needed help. The guy who gave it to me was long-suffering with idiots, kind with his words, and generous with his time and tools. This is because he loves bikes. He loves restoring them. It's not his main job but a decent second income. It's like having a hobby you adore. If they let you, you'll talk to people all day long about it. Got someone who is interested in your beloved hobby? You'll give them all the time they need to share what you have already learned. He did. He was easy and generous with fools; I was their undisputed king. I know as much about engines as the average goat knows about, well, engines. I know a lot more now, and I am still learning because of this older man who will gladly teach—for free. Why are we all not like that with our jobs?

Just to help solidify what I mean, I'd have to tell you about a wrench, or at least the need for the proper wrench. I have bought and sold several houses I worked on and made a good profit. I had to build the tools to do all these side jobs. I was at home in the garage puttering about on the bike and its pieces, and I just couldn't seem to get a good fit on this one nut I had to remove. Working on a bike over fifty years old is hard enough without rust seizing bolts and nuts like they were supposed to be welded down. I couldn't just meat-fist this thing, and an adjustable wrench would not do the trick because you need the right size.

I have a good set of wrenches. Whether you know a lot about tools or not, you probably know there are standard sizes, like ¾, ½, and the like. You probably also know there are metric tools like 10mm, 11mm, blah, blah, blah. I have all those—both sets in ratchet and wrenches. However, no matter what I used, there was too much wiggle. Whatever I did, I could get close but not fitted. I was at a dead stop, so I broke down and called my friend. He knew the issue before I finished describing the problem. It's called experience, and he has it squirting out of his ears. If I could just get him to wear buckets that hang off his head, I could capture and use or sell this experience juice. In the meantime, I have to ask for much-needed help.

"You need a Whitworth," he said.

"What in the name of all that's holy is a..." I tried to get out.

15

"It's a wrench size for English bikes from a certain period. I have more than one set. I'll drop some off for you that you can borrow."

He knew the issue, was more than well prepared, and brought them to me to borrow. That is a super-specialist.

Those insurance agents who wouldn't stop and help me with my issues taught us a lot about how we should interact with our clients and a great deal about how a business can't rely on their merchant statement for real, understandable information. Buying homes, upgrading them, and slowly restoring that British bike has given me a decent set of tools. They also taught me that the absolute worst tool a human being can have is not the wrong tool; it's the almost right tool.

A wrong tool can be put down quickly because it's the wrong tool. The almost-right tool will make you scream and swear obscenities with such vehemence that your spouse will grab the children (all the children—theirs and anyone else's in the neighborhood), stuff their ears with wax, and drive them to the Klondike for a three-day adventure "while Daddy finishes up."

A merchant statement says it's the tool for the job, looks like the tool for the job, and will make you pull out a calculator, slide rule, and abacus and Google every third abbreviation to try to decipher it. It generally doesn't work because it's almost the right tool. When all those spent man-hours do work, it's just as effective as getting you to put it down because you don't want to have to do that every month. Not to mention that the statements change their look and layout every six to eight months for *just this reason*. They want you to put it down, put it in a drawer, and put it out of your mind. It's working, right? The money is going into your account, right? Then don't worry your precious little head over it, sweetheart.

3

TEACH ME, MASTER

Now, can I teach you to read this? Yes. Well, no, not really. Not unless you move into our offices for three weeks and do a few hundred of these for eight or so hours a day while we bring you coffee. I *can* teach you how to do a little self-assessment that will be a great fuel gauge for you to see how well you're doing. And let's face it. Do you want to become an expert in every field you may have to interact with? No, you don't. You want to develop specialists who do that all day long for you. Still, being able to see it overall at a glance is helpful. Let's get into that.

This tool will work whatever your industry. First, understand that in the world of merchant accounts, businesses are split into two groups: card present and card not present. Understand that well. The second thing is that it all rides on levels of risk—just like insurance. I know, I know. I hate to go back to that, but it works here, not at the specialist level of insurance, but the basic idea. The riskier something is, the more expensive it is to get insured, right? The guy who drives a Corvette pays more than the guy who drives a Chevette. If you don't understand that, look up pictures of a Chevette. You'll understand why, in college, the kids said they were pieces of Shi-vit. A Corvette could drive through a shopping mall

17

without slowing noticeably. A Chevette will almost make it to the bottom of a hill with a tailwind.

Card present means exactly that. The card is physically there at the business and is swiped, tapped, waved, or whatever. In other words, retail. A storefront business. Card not present means, of course, that the card is not at the business. These include over the phone, online, and some businesses that might be confusing, like gyms. A gym may seem like a retail shop. You're there at the gym, and your wallet or purse is with you. But you don't swipe it. It's on file, and they bill you monthly. That makes it card not present.

It's also important to understand that a merchant account has numerous fees. We'll boil this down to a merchant account reduction sauce to simplify it and make what is called an effective rate, which will be a percentage. It sounds daunting, but I promise, if you do it only a couple of times, you'll master it. Use makes mastery. Do it every month, and your merchant account provider will not understand how you stay on top of it all. They'll pull out smoke and mirrors and say, "Nothing up my sleeves." You'll counter with, "Keep my number here or under, or there will be nothing in my account with your group."

4

THIRTY—AS IN THIRTY

The two big fees in a merchant account hot in each and every transaction. The discount rate (which is a percentage) and a per transaction fee (a flat number, generally a few cents). Why multiple numbers? There are many reasons, but the real reason is the industry type and how much money they make.

I once started a consultation with a potential client. I had a good chance of getting my daily fee (large) plus travel and expenses, which normally included a large steak as they were a $30-million-per-year business. Nothing dirty there, as they wanted a specialist they could trust who would come in, sort out the haywire, give them a streamlined account, and explain how to do it—three days max. I could taste the steak. This was pre-2005, so there were no Zoom accounts and all that. A plane would be involved.

Sadly for me, I fixed their issues in under ten minutes on that first call. No steak. You see, they needed credit card processing software. That was a specialty of mine. The first thing in the basic interview was to see what they were doing. Could he give me some basics in terms of how much they did per month, per week, or per day so I could build out some basics? Nothing too intense, just anything off the top of his head.

"Well, I told you," he said.

"Forgive me. I missed it. Please, tell me again," I replied.

"Thirty million per year."

"Yes, sir, but how many transactions?"

"Thirty. We do thirty $1 million transactions a year." Okay, I'm screwed. Not really, but no steak. I could solve this now. Without being prompted by my ethics angel on my shoulder and while my steak devil was showing what I would miss out on, I told him the facts.

I knew he was looking for a $28,000 piece of software to handle this, but he did not need it. He could do it for under a few hundred. But he insisted that he must have the big software since he did $30 million in sales. That's when we (We? I. I am not the queen.) laid out that it wasn't the dollar amount the software handled; it was the number of transactions. He had to think of it like eggs in a basket. Twenty- to thirty-thousand-dollar software would handle three thousand eggs a day and up. One for about five hundred dollars would handle up to one thousand eggs a day. He needed to do thirty eggs per year. (What the hell was he selling, anyway? Gold yachts? Death lasers? Volcano fortresses? How many evil scientists could one firm have for clients, anyway?)

The poor little millionaire was actually a little dejected. "Are you sure?"

"Sir, if I was wrong, you wouldn't want my consultation anyway. You have thirty eggs to do a year. That's not even three transactions a month. I'd love the trip and steak dinner, but you have an easy fix. I know forty companies that do less than a third of what you do and have no choice but to spend twenty to thirty thousand. You have a good problem. If it helps, just send me an Omaha steak for the fix, and call me when you have anything else come up like this."

Why do I tell you this? The average retail transaction fee on a credit card is around 1.70 percent. It should be lower, but that's an average. A per transaction fee, sometimes called an authorization fee or auth fee, is $0.18. On a $1 million transaction, a change of one basis point (one one-hundredth of a percentage), or going from 1.70 percent to 1.71 percent, is $100. If this guy had 1.71 percent and should have 1.61 percent, he would overpay $1,000 every time a card came in. However, he would never notice if he was raked over the coals with a per transaction fee of $5.00 instead of $0.18. That's not a flea on an elephant. It's a flea on a mountain.

Instead, if we look at a convenience store (often called a C-Store in the biz), they have foot traffic of four hundred-plus people per day with $10 transactions. They'll never notice if they go from 1.70 percent to 1.78 percent. However, if they go from their incredibly low per-transaction fee of generally $0.05 to the normal $0.18, they would have to close their doors in a month.

So, we understand there are two fees in every transaction. The discount (percentage) and a per trans (flat number). Now, we add the other three hundred little ankle-biter fees that eat us out of house and home—the monthly fee, the reporting fee, the PCI compatibility fee (assuming you haven't gone PCI non-compliant), and a host of others. It makes it hard to avoid the mistakes of my old insurance rep and keep it simple. Right? No. We can make it one fee. It will be imperfect, but it is still a good gauge.

Some people will balk at that and say, "Even a wrong clock is right twice a day, but that's not really *telling time*, is it?" No, that would not be the case, but a speedometer that is off a couple of miles can keep you from getting a ticket. Actually, it can't keep you from getting the ticket, but it can help your brain know it should slow down. It's your lead foot you have to worry about.

An effective rate will be all things rolled into one dough to get us one single percentage. It will be higher than your discount rate in almost every case, but it will tell you a one-dough percentage. It puts everything together and kneads it into a homogenous whole. To do it, one first needs the total amount in credit and debit card sales for the month. Second, we need the total fees taken out. This part can get tricky. I have taught this for a while, and a lot of groups break up their fees to look abnormally low. Dirty pool? Yes. Legal? Yes. As long as it's there, it's legal. Don't worry; there's a simple trick to know if you have everything.

All you need is a calculator that works and a finger. Divide your total fees by your total sales.

Total Fees ÷ Total Sales = _____

We're not done yet. This is a decimal, but it's not your percentage. This fact alone is used to keep many businesses overpaying every month and all year/ career long. I had a man call me—a real no-nonsense type. "Just wanted my rates." I didn't want to speak like my old insurance guy. (*I really have nothing against insurance people, just that one person. Please don't groan. I now have people I rely on heavily, and they treat me how I like. Because of this, I refer others to them. Referrals show the greatest trust and are the greatest compliment you can give a business.*) But I needed a little more.

He worked in retail. I had to make sure, though. Yes, his customers had their credit cards and swiped them on-site. No, he was not in a risk category. I hate blind quoting someone and thus have to give the caveat that if other facts come out, it could change the rate. I know people like blind quotes because it's easy to think that if I see his statement, I could just squeeze under his old number and not give him a good rate, just a slightly better one. So, I quoted him. I told him he would probably get 1.61 percent and $0.18 per transaction.

That's when he flipped his lid.

"Whoa, whoa, *whoa!* That's *way* more than I thought it would be. Glad I asked. You'd retire off my account, and I'd be screwed!" His language, not mine. Sorry.

"Sir, I quoted you and put a good foot forward. Since you won't go with me anyway, do you mind telling me where you're at right now? Do you have a statement in front of you? Maybe something in the industry changed in the last two days." (The was obviously off his rocker.) I replied, knowing it was a good rate.

"Heck, yes, I do. My statement is in front of me, and I am glad it is because I only pay (*wait for it!*) 0.03125 percent!" Oh, you could hear the satisfaction in his voice. I was obviously some shyster who took widow's money from them and forced them to eat cat food to survive. If only my parents had been married, I could get out of the leisure suit and gold medallions on my chest, get rid of the slick-backed hair, and be a professional.

"Sir?"

"Yes," he replied triumphantly, knowing I'd been caught red-handed like a merchant account pirate deep in my skullduggery.

"Let's make sure. How much were your sales—your total sales for the month?"

"$20,000 and some change." It was still there in his voice. He was the guy who beat the villain.

"Oh, good. You're doing well. That's always good. Can you tell me what your total fees for the month were?" I asked.

"Yep," very smug. "They were $625 and some change."

At this point, dear reader, I do *not* need a calculator (and soon, neither will you) to know—and I mean like the hand of God slapping on the Earth itself to *know*—that $625 is more, *way more* than one-third of 1 percent of $20,000. One percent would be $200. A third of that would be $63 bucks.

If this guy thinks he is getting away with only paying $63 on $20,000, he's out of his gourd.

"Sir, that is not a percentage."

"What isn't a percentage?" he asked.

"The 0.03125 you quoted me. That's only one-third of 1 percent. You *know* $625 is not less than one-third of 1 percent of $20,000. You'd have to change it to a percentage. You have to move the decimal two times to the right (some of you are having nausea thinking of sixth-grade math right now) to get a percentage. It looks like you're paying 3.12 percent."

Slight hesitation. The edifice of his heroism for cowardly crook-catching was getting shaky.

"That's not right," he said, unsure of himself. Mostly because I hadn't faltered once in the conversation, no matter his triumph. I had neither stammered nor backed out of the conversation. Wouldn't a crook do that?

"Sir, I'll teach you a trick you can use forever. You don't know me from Adam, but dividing your total fees from your total sales means you'll get that 0.03125. The issue is it's not a percentage (dang, that sixth-grade math!). You then have to multiply it by one hundred or simply move the decimal two places to the right," I told him, assured but not cocky. The guy had been overpaying, and there was no reason to beat a man about to see all his losses.

"That's not right," he said. The poor guy was stuck in a loop.

"Sir, you *know* that $625 is not less than 1 percent of $20,000. One percent would be like two hundred bucks."

"That's not right," he was using a calculator now. I could hear it click-clacking.

"It's okay. Test my math. Multiply 20,000 by 3 percent. What do you get? I get six hundred. You're paying $625 on $20,000, or 3.12 percent."

That's when I removed the phone from my ear by a couple of feet. Apparently, for some unknown reason, his treasonous and highly ungrateful calculator agreed with me, forgetting all he had done for it through the years. There was swearing involved. Also, I think a couple of things were hit or thrown; however, I can't firmly attest to what happened. But there was movement and loud sounds. I can firmly attest to the swearing, though. Firmly.

I apologized for my industry. I do that a lot. A lot. That's also the next step in the training. You need to move the decimal. Here's where we were:

Total Fees ÷ Total Sales = _____

Now, let's look at that with Loud Guy.

625 ÷ 20,000 = 0.03125

But that's not the answer yet. That number just gets us to:

Swearing + Hitting and/or Throwing =
(innocent items)

So, we have to move the decimal two spaces to the right or multiply by one hundred:

625 ÷ 20,000 = 003.125

Then, the math is done, and we add the symbol to express it as a percentage. (Fancy!)

625 ÷ 20,000 = 003.125%

Congratulations on being 20,000 leagues ahead of 99.9 percent of businesses out there. If you do this monthly, you'll stay there.

But we have to apply it. We must have an idea of where it goes and where it should be. A shaky speedometer that's off by two miles per hour can only keep you from getting a ticket if you 1) heed its advice and 2) know the speed limit for where you're driving.

5

BIGGER DOESN'T MEAN BETTER: THE $1 MILLION A MONTH CAR DEALERSHIP

I was in front of a car dealership. It was better than average, you might say. They were doing a little under $1 million a month in plastic transactions alone. I know, I know. They're suffering. Pray for them. They've grown since.

And before you ask, no. They don't really sell cars on credit and debit cards. Their plastic sales are all behind-the-counter stuff—parts, services, oil changes, and extended warranties. It's what is often referred to as the movie theater model. It's not the ticket for the new superhero movie that gets you; it's the popcorn, soda, etc. What are Jujubes and Sno-Caps anyway?

These guys were introduced to us by a nonprofit we consulted with. That's the best. But they had warned us and the person from the nonprofit. Not to make them sound vain, but they simply said, "We're big. We have a small army of bookkeepers. We have chased off ten bank reps in the past twelve months because we have a great rate." No, they didn't really chase people off. They meant they would tell reps that they had a great rate. (Of course, they did. They had three hundred employees; they were bona fide.) And the reps would be defeated and leave without challenging it. Many salespeople are shaking their heads right now at this truth.

My in-person answer to the nonprofit lead was simple. Great. Pretend God comes down and says they'll never go with us. Pretend their brother-in-law, who can't keep a job elsewhere, has the account, and they'll be on the couch if they switch. Have us do a rate review anyway. If they have a great rate, it'll confirm it. They can have the report with the red ink for free if they don't. The brother-in-law may have the account, but he doesn't get to retire on it. In short, use us to keep an honest man honest.

They were overpaying.

Their self-assuredness hurt them because reps believed them when they said they had a really good rate. They left. And the dealership had money on the table. Still, my plan worked with the rate review against the brother-in-law example. They went for it and submitted a chain of statements.

I'll never forget that meeting. It was the third account I was ever introduced by a nonprofit, and they were overpaying almost $23,000 a year. The GM, the big, *big* GM, was in that meeting on that fateful day, as was his chief bookkeeper. He said, "Wow, that's a car. That's a whole car."

"Well, you should know," I said, since they were a car dealership, and we all had a big laugh. It was fun. Now, I had two jobs going into that meeting, and they were as follows:

1. Get the account

2. Don't get the head bookkeeper fired for doing his job and not knowing *mine*.

As it turns out, they were and are a wonderfully ethical company. His job was never in jeopardy. Still, I took the time. I walked them through how this is not a gaping wound but death by a thousand pinpricks. They were slowly being bled, but they originally had a pretty good rate. That's when I told them how the bookkeeper could keep my firm honest with the effective rate calculation.

"You should be paying in the 1.6 percent range on a standard credit card and less than 1 percent on a debit card as it's even safer—something like 0.87 percent," I told them.

"Where are we now?" asked the big, *big* GM.

"2.24 percent," I said hesitantly, "on both."

They were not only paying a higher rate but also had left the card-present rates and gotten into the riskier and thus more expensive rates of the card-not-present accounts. Time to jump in. It was not the bookkeeper's fault. If you ask your car mechanic to fix the engine in your boat, he'll get the basic ideas, but boats have their idiosyncrasies. You'll have bigger boat issues later. Here's where these numbers had half of their damage hidden. This is where the debit card started creeping up. Also, don't try to memorize this.

"Why not?" asked the bookkeeper.

"This layout will change shortly. They never leave one footprint in place for long," I told them. They started seeing the strategy used against them. It started to make sense. No reason for X-marks-the-spot on shifting sands. "Besides," I smiled, "You have your own specialist in me. Now, we will track it for you. And I'll show you how to roll all this gobbledygook of numbers into one dough. The effective rate can be used on one location or the whole. We call it the Sixty-Second Audit."

That's when we showed them the speed limit to judge against. As a retail organization, they shouldn't be over 2 percent for an effective rate. While we do a much deeper dive when going over statements for different companies, even we use the effective rate calculation for a quick glance. It's a view from 30,000 feet. It doesn't tell you the details but helps you see what's happening. You'll see if there is fire, invaders from

Mars, whatever. You'll have no idea what kind of ordinance invaders from Mars are carrying. For that, you need a specialist, but you'll do much better knowing something.

Let's go back to our math for just a moment and see what we're talking about. Below is the blank:

$$\text{Total Fees} \div \text{Total Sales} = \underline{\hspace{2cm}}$$

Our starting point, per usual. Let's add Loud Guy's numbers, as we are familiar with that whole train wreck.

$$625 \div 20{,}000 = 003.125\%$$

Okay, we have our effective rate, but is it good or bad? First, we have to define our position. Is this a retail business? Card present? Yes. No oddities or risk? No. Standard bill of fare only. Regular retail store. Goodie, then our attack should be based on the 2 percent marker. A retail location should be at or below 2 percent as an effective rate.

$$\text{Effective Rate} \le 2\% = \text{Happy Business Owner}$$

Now, his numbers were:

$$625 \div 20{,}000 = 3.125\%$$

Unfortunately, as we have discovered:

$$3.125\% > 2\% = \text{Swearing} + \text{Throwing/Crashing}$$

6

TRAPS, TRAPS, AND TRAPS

This one time, I almost got fired—almost. If you're very sensitive and can't deal with being let down again, I'll give you a spoiler alert: I kept the client. You see, a call came in one fine day as I was in my air-conditioned office. After pleasantries, which were literally and figuratively being phoned in, I realized this customer wasn't happy. In fact, the call was going in the direction of your basic Dear John letter. Was she breaking up with me? We were so good together. It wasn't me. She was happy with me. I was fine. It wasn't her either. No, it was the processor we put her with. She liked us but never felt like she was being treated as she should when she called the processor. She put all her cards on the table. She was leaving and was informing me. That's when I asked her a question that she had not prepared for in any way.

"Would you like me to fire that processor?"

What was I talking about? Really? Could that be done? I can do that. You can do that?! People don't expect a response like mine in a world full of business responses that are more "the company line" and have a lot of things in them like, "Well, at this time," and are more about saving the company face than taking care of the client. News flash: The client is how you make money. Don't chop up the goose laying the golden eggs. Feed it. Love it.

"You better believe that I can do it. I don't work for them; I work for you. If you don't like them, I *hate* them. I can put you with another processor, and if you don't like them, I can fire them, too." I went on and told her how it wouldn't cost her a dime, and we handle all the paperwork. And that's what we did. I explained that, unlike most, I don't work with one group but numerous. I told her to think of me like an independent insurance agent. (See, I can be nice to those guys.) I represent many processors and acquirers. Most are good, some okay, and some not so great. I only place the three biggest dogs on the block, but if something odd comes down the pipeline, I have a wide net.

We moved her medical practice. She was happy, and the new processor took good care of her. All was well in the world. The underlying problem was she was pretty sure that we (and she, by default) were locked in. In many cases, she would have been right. Freedom of movement is freedom, period.

The issue here is that most people get their merchant account from a bank. A bank generally has a charter with a single processor. You tell me what bank you use, and I can normally tell you your processor. No kidding. But if we go back to our nice doctor lady who called to Dear John me, what could I have done if I had only signed for that one processor she didn't like? "Well, you see, Ma'am, at this point in time, we are currently only representing at this juncture... the processor who couldn't seem to care what's going on with you."

Ever had this kind of answer? Who teaches this garbage?

Guess what the first order of business is when you don't want customers to be unhappy with you? Fix it so they are happy? That is *one* option, but in business, it'd be better at this point in time, per se, to just make it where they *can't read their statement.*

7

PITFALLS: CREEP

There is no way around this statement other than to just blurt it out. I don't care what the person says, what you signed, or who you know in the industry. *Your rate will go up.* That is true. And the few times it's not, it's doubly true. It's extra true. It's going up, that's it.

"But I have a contract!" Faust did as well and look how that worked out. That contract, which is often three or four pages of basic stuff and twelve to eighteen pages of fine print (now which is commonly replaced with: "I agree with the Terms of Service as stated on the www.this-rate-is-going-up.com's website.") Those extra pages and Terms of Service basically depict that if a fly sneezes anywhere in time and space of the known or unknown universe, your rate can and will go up. It'd be sad if it wasn't so blatantly obvious. That's why you don't get a letter, email, or quarterly message from the firm's president stating the uptick. You get small, incremental pops that are hard to notice but do great damage.

There's an old tale of an eagle that flew to a mountain. It landed and started pecking at the side. The mountain laughed and laughed at the wee little bird and said he was a mountain. What could one small squab do? The bird pecked though and pecked, and the mountain, sure of his safety, never saw the eagle slowly chiseling through until his demise.

Not your average Aesop's Fable, to be sure. I think it's Middle Eastern in origin, but in this case, it's the mountain chiseling away at smaller businesses and bleeding them dry. Your rate can and will go up—as well known by my father.

My dad is a good businessman in his own right. He's tough, shrewd, and generous with his staff and demands they do a better job than anyone he competes with. If he has to let someone go, he does it as quickly as possible, and because of how he treats them, he has staff members who've been with him for decades. The Bible says that even a prophet does not get honor in his own village, and I, ladies and gentlemen, am no prophet. Still, it took me more than two months to get my father to let me review his statements for one of his side businesses.

"I have a great rate. I argued this rate for two months," he told me. I then explained what he made an hour and that he wasted his time if he spent two months arguing. He finally relented (though I know a lot of dads who would have given the statements the same day the son asked. Just saying.) and stood there proudly as the kid he knew—who flew around the house with a towel for a cape and made webs for his action figures—stood and glanced over his statements. He was a businessman, after all. He had numerous accounts with that bank. How was his kid (who was now an adult and had already spent years in the industry working to bring credit card processing software to the market) going to beat the bank that he beat up to get that rate?

"Two grand."

"Two grand what?" he asked.

"Two grand. You are overpaying two grand a year. Now, it's a small store, mind you, and I don't have a calculator here in your living room. But at a glance, it's at least two grand," I said.

"How? I argued that rate over two months."

"You make too much an hour to spend two months on anything other than keeping someone alive. Why argue with them? If you felt they weren't giving you a good rate, I don't know, a week into the discussion, leave."

"I have a contract," he said, getting louder—obviously, a bit embarrassed that maybe he should have listened to the kid in the towel a little earlier.

I explained the contract that Faust signed with Mephisto. I explained that what he signed was *not* a lease on an apartment with a fixed rental rate but that the rate could and did go up. When he signed, he had an almost perversely low rate. A rate so low that if I could sell it now, I'd make a million dollars a day because inflation has passed that. He was paying 3.1 percent for a discount rate at a retail store—not a 3.1 percent effective rate, but 3.1 percent on a standard credit card. He was quite literally in the lower rates for adult material, which is something my firm won't even handle.

I didn't want to beat Daddy up, but he was done. He signed the next day, and I have watched his accounts for him ever since. He is my dad, after all. If I do it for all the other businesses, I am surely going to do it for him. He's saved well over $30,000, as that was fifteen years ago at the time of this writing. But that's what those monies do. They creep up and up. That creep makes all the people up the food chain get a bigger and bigger piece of your pie. If you don't think it will, it already has. If you saw it in the past and fixed the leak, it has come back in a new way.

Creep is the single driving thing that we push home every day. That's why I hire specialists, and it is why people hire my firm. It's hard to watch everything every day. I spend *no* time worrying about my AC. I have a guy. He checks it out quarterly. Could something spring up in between those times? Certainly, but that problem will find me. In the meantime, he'll find all the small things I can't (and flat won't) look for. Same with my pool and same with my insurance.

The best tool against creep is 1) a specialist and 2) the effective fate equation. Learning the second one helps keep the first one honest. It also makes it so that when you think you have a specialist, the effective rate equation will prove it over time. Little hits will pop up, but with a specialist, you'll see them go back down.

8

THE DEVIL IS IN THE NUMBERS

I recently consulted for a humane society. I love charity and think it is a double-coupon day for the soul. You give and feel good; they get the blessing and take it into their community. What's not to love? Besides, no matter what broken road you've gone down in your life, there is a charity that speaks to your heart. Go look. If you don't see it, start it.

I have spoken to numerous humane societies, Habitats for Humanity, Goodwill, and the Salvation Army. These places are in their own field because they are both nonprofits and nonprofit retail locations that help fund them. Most of the time, there are savings, but they are not necessarily huge. The system can be good to nonprofits, but that isn't always the case.

One of the most recent cases I reviewed for a humane society was an account that did $17,500 in their storefront in one month. It wasn't huge, but they are a local nonprofit. This amount includes adoptions, shots, donations, and the whole nine yards. The issue was even though their rate looked really good at a glance, too much was coming out. When we dove deeper, it was worse than we had thought. It was so bad that we sent the data to a processor and said, "Check our math," hoping we were wrong. Sometimes, being wrong is good. Instead, we were dead on. They were overpaying $9,900 annually, or a hundred bucks shy of $10,000 a year.

By way of comparison, remember that $1 million a month car dealership that I saved $23,000 a year? Does that sound impressive? To be on the same scale, I would need to have saved that dealership $571,000 a year—not $23,000. If $23,000 was "a whole car," $571,000 was a whole fleet of vehicles. It is simply the worst thing in this vein I have ever seen. Remember that I wrote a column for a business paper entitled "The Year in Fraud," where I listed the obscene things people did with merchant accounts every January. This one wins.

When we discussed this with the processors, they asked twice, "This is a charity? This is a charity's account?" Yes. Then came a one-word answer: "Despicable."

The real issue was this wasn't the same ole, same ole creep. This was a padded number. In twenty years, I have never seen anything like it. I've seen padded, but not this. First, one has to know there is a type of account that is very common these days called an interchange plus account. Interchange is almost (it's not, but almost) like wholesale. No, you can't get an account at interchange + 0—not even close. Dream about being Superman, as it's more likely.

You'll notice that it's written as interchange and a plus (+) symbol. Even more often as IC+ and then whatever is added. Here's the issue. This is a creep system designed to hide numbers not from you but from me. This is because when we see IC+20, we know where the account is at. We know it. It's like glancing at an analog watch without trying to really read it.

Do you know how they keep elephants from busting out of the circus? It is a sad tale to tell. Elephants are the biggest, strongest thing in the jungle. Elephants uproot some tree types by simply leaning in and pushing until the seemingly immovable tree gives way to the elephant's irresistible force. Elephants also have, as we know, very strong memories. They recognize other elephants from multiple decades ago, as well as people. So, how do they keep them from busting out of the circus? They put a shackle on their back foot attached to a rope that is tied to a small stake in the ground. But that doesn't add up, does it? If you can push a tree down, you can get a small wooden stake out of the ground or at least break the rope.

Here's what was done *in the past*: When the elephant was a wee calf, they put a strong shackle around one of its rear ankles and then chain it with a fairly stout chain to a long iron bar hammered six feet or so into the ground. The calf tries and tries to break the chain but can't. Eventually, the chain breaks him. Not to be overly maudlin, but elephants actually cry. They not only cry out, but elephants cry tears. The calf learns that the chain cannot be broken and gives in to the shackle. Once this is done, no matter how big he grows, he will "know" that he cannot break it. All he needs is the simple reminder of a small shackle, a rope, and a small wooden stake to give him a small resistance to his rear foot. As he knows he cannot break it, he does not try.

True story.

I tell you this because we had to train people. Really, we had to retrain them. We had to retrain them to look for this insidious device. Why? Because no one looks at the IC part of the IC+ account. They look for the number after the plus sign. They look at the thirty in IC+30. The thirty is the important part. The thirty is what we can work with. The rest is set by MC/Visa and the system. Not today. On this account, we saw when we dove deep, and I mean we were swimming to China, that the IC, the Interchange rate itself, had been padded. It was not padded a little; it was padded to the point where they were paying basically 7 percent on a standard credit card and had an effective rate of almost 8 percent when all was said and done. And they are a charity.

Despicable is right.

I don't like to oversell something. Don't get me wrong; if we sit down at a get-together with nachos and a beer or a charcuterie board and a pitcher of sangria, *mon frere*, I will spin you a tale that will hang over your house like an epic poem of Greek heroes by Homer himself. But when it comes to me helping your business, especially your nonprofit business, I have to give you brass tacks, even when bad. In this case, I had to hold back from pouring over the absolute treachery of it all for no other reason than I sound like a snake oil salesman. It was bad—that bad. Yes. Bedside manner here meant everything. This would also be great training for the team. Do not be the elephant. Don't "know" anything. Go effective rate for a glance, then swim for the bottom—each time, every time. The numbers will tell.

9

TRAPPED BY A KILLER MACHINE

Machines are great. They make our lives easier. But anything can be a trap. Ask Admiral Ackbar. In this case, it was a merchant that I couldn't beat the rate. I couldn't match it. That doesn't happen. I mean, it absolutely does not happen. The best—the *best*—rate someone can get, I can match. This one I couldn't, and that dog won't hunt, *Monsignor*. Again, a deep dive led us to one, inescapable conclusion: they were paying less than cost—less, as in it was costing their group money every time they ran a card. That dog also does not hunt. For that matter, that dog doesn't exist. Nobody pays a business to run plastic.

We swam deeper this time. We had to go into extra detail. Was there anything else? There was no machine cost in here. Did they have a separate cost coming out of their business checking account? Pay dirt. They did.

Now, for the women readers, I have to explain something here, as not all women know the game King of the Hill. You may have heard of the show, but that was a play on words for a guy whose last name was Hank Hill. No, the game King of the Hill. I have noticed that all men, and just about 50 percent of women, know. Don't be upset. It's because you're not idiots. That's what King of the Hill is: a game of idiots. When boys

41

are left alone—in any quantity—we do dumb things. That's why the Bible says, "He that findeth a wife, findeth a good thing," because we're idiots. A wife, most fiancés, and many steady girlfriends who are planning a future with a guy will step in when we want to do something stupid and say, "No, you are *not* getting a free trip to the ER tonight with your idiot friends." See, that's a good thing. Wives have been preserving humanity for years. In the South, we have the famous last words of idiot guys being, "Hey, y'all! Check this out!"

King of the Hill is a game that boys play. You find any high spot in the yard, be it a slight mound, old tire, dead body, or whatever you have. You get on top of it (sometimes as much as four inches higher than the rest of the area) and say, "I'm King of the Hill!" Then, every other idiot boy in the yard rushes up and pushes, shoves, grabs, claws, bites, scratches, and claws to be the one to get to the top of the hill and hold it from the other invading barbarian kings known as your idiot friends. Yes, ladies, shake your heads. This is what boys do. It's like watching a bunch of caffeinated goats run about and butt heads. I did this. I didn't watch, people. I participated. Gladly. Idiot. Now, what invariably happens is that one kid who is already shaving by second grade takes and holds the hill. After a bit, there is a sweaty, panting, laughing bunch of idiot boys piled on the ground living their best-bruised lives.

King of the Hill. Idiots.

So, when there is a whiteboard section in our office in the public conference area marked King of the Hill with a dollar amount under it, the team stops and asks what is up. What's up is that was where we started writing the dollar amount for the single most expensive amount per month we have seen charged to a company for a small, cheap, easily purchased black box credit card terminal. We had all seen $35, $38, then $48, and even $54 a month for a machine that was $200 out of the box—brand new. Then, we saw $62, $72, and even $75. The other numbers moved quickly. They couldn't hold the hill long. But $75 stayed a while until it was dethroned by $99—$99 per month. Unfortunately, we are now getting into leases.

A lease is the dirtiest thing you can do to a human being. Leases are generally unbreakable. The number of leases I have seen cross my desk from potential clients titled "Unbreakable Lease Agreement" breaks my heart. Imagine charging people ungodly sums for the cheapest of commodities via unbreakable contracts. They are four-year agreements, meaning the $99-per-month lease charges someone $1,200 per year— $4,800 over four years—and the business doesn't even own it at the end of the agreement. They can now buy the $200 terminal for $1,800, and they have already paid $4,800 for its use.

Sound good? Does anyone want to sign up for that?

Well, that $99 was finally dethroned. The usurper was $142 a month. To date, that is the grand heavy-weight champion, and rightly so. This company would pay $6,816 for their machine. The company that held the lease also set up its merchant account. The account was almost $50 below cost every month and was being grossly overcharged $142 a month for a $200 machine to make up for the difference—four years, locked in, no backsies. This is when you have to lay out that a business has cancer of the merchant account. We didn't sign the client, as it could only do them damage. They were locked in. They had to pay that obscene—I'll repeat, that obscene—rate. We had the date it would come to an end and had to contact them a few months before. We would have to remind them that they would not even own the machine for the almost $7,000 they paid, so don't get back into bed with these guys for any reason.

43

This game of three-card Monty is done every day. Today, it's a lease; tomorrow, the machine belongs to the processor, and if you leave, you lose it. (So what? They're basically free and often are.)

Here is what you need to do. Think of this like getting a cell phone. It will make you wary and simplify it. We've all asked ourselves: I'm here getting a cell plan and phone. Are they going to fleece me on the phone or the plan?

The best thing is that almost any company in the world would give you a phone, maybe not the best phone, but a phone if you sign up for the plan. That's where they make their money. Keep reading, and you'll see what I mean about gas stations. The difference is that there are few exceptions on credit card terminals in terms of basic versus fancy. Unlike a phone that can have many options, credit card terminals are never going to take your picture for a selfie. When they do, I'm leaving the planet.

Certain things are fungible. This is a great term to understand. It's an easily replaceable item. The teddy bear you loved till half the fuzz came off pulling a full-on Velveteen Rabbit story was absolutely not fungible. If your mom had three extras of those teddies in the closet, knowing you would all but destroy one, it wasn't interchangeable. That one—that very one—was yours and yours alone. No other version would do. Not fungible.

A credit card terminal is the very definition of fungible. You can replace it three times a week and not care as long as it runs and the money goes to your account. In other words, a terminal is a terminal is a terminal. It isn't worth paying more for it, getting trapped in a contract, and being unable to switch your merchant account when they own your terminal. There's no reason to get locked into such nonsense. You can literally get on eBay and buy one today. If it's marked at $1, understand it's a trap. All you need to know is: Does it run, and is it locked? Locked is a real thing. Make it a part of your determination process, but at the end of the day, if you are already running and need a new terminal, your new processor will gladly give you a terminal if you switch to them.

Just like a cell phone.

10

THE OLD LADY AND THE LEASE... SOON

U nfortunately, that's not as bad as it gets. The $99 a month was actually worse than the $142, and I'll tell you why for the sole purpose of explaining the steal. Knowing how they steal is important so you can get around it. We'll get to it. Fear not. But first, let us speak of the dreaded POS.

11

THE POINT-OF-SALE PITFALL

Point-of-sale systems are normally referred to as POS because we're lazy, and it sounds cooler. Remember that realtors call roaches *palmetto bugs*. You can buy a house with palmetto bugs, but you might not buy a house with giant cockroaches so big you can put a saddle on them and ride. See the difference? One can come up with a euphemism for anything. These are handy and worthwhile devices, but with a lie like a palmetto bug, you can have a big ugly thing in your business you hate, no matter the name.

I know a millionaire. He's kind of like a millionaire's millionaire. He builds gas stations and all but gives them away. He doesn't care about it at all. He does care about the *fuel rights,* though. That's a big, big deal to him. When you buy a gas station from him for almost nothing, you sign a contract saying that he will have the fuel rights for your store forever. Forever. The store can make a family money, and thus, they want it. The gas they sell will also make them money, and they must buy all the gas from him. So, he has many gas stations without the need to run them with all their day-to-day management, and all buy gas from him. It's not a new idea. Have you ever heard of this little place called McDonald's? They don't go to Walmart to buy beef.

POS are great to have; you just have to know where the leaks are. The big one is, of course, the merchant account. Can you switch it? Is there a fee to do so? There are so many POS systems that lock in the merchant account because, just like the fuel rights, there is a lot of money to be made. I consulted for a company that paid $10,000 for a POS. Their merchant account was locked in, so they didn't feel much consultation was needed, and they didn't want to get a new POS. After all, they had spent all that money on the one they have now. That's when you earn your stripes and remind them that's exactly why you dig through. It turns out that they were overpaying $6,000 a year for the past four years. They had thus gotten a POS that cost them an additional $24,000 (and would cost them a total of $30,000 if they didn't switch). They did feel a little carsick but were wiser for the wear.

If you can't switch your merchant account, you will feel like that baby elephant with a big old shackle on your ankle and no way to break it. Know before going in.

12

THE GREATEST LIE OF ALL TIME: THERE IS NO CONTRACT

"The other guy said that his company had no contract," the business owner said. We sat there together with his wife at their fledgling coffee shop. This is not my first rodeo; when you do something every day, you can't be tricked. You're not winging it like someone working on a couple of bullet points when you have the *Encyclopedia Britannica* rolling about in your head. I did not laugh.

If you have children of almost any age, you know (or soon will learn) about helping them learn to read. My daughter was very funny about this. She would sound out the words, slowly trudging through the easiest material in the world for me as an adult. Then, as she tired in her brain pan, she would flat out stop trying and guess a wrong, really bad guess at a word. "Sit" is not "laughing," and I (and you) could never be confused. I would say, "Baby, that's not the word," and she would argue.

"I think that's the word, Daddy."

"No, it's not," I'd reply.

"But..."

"Lillie, Daddy has been reading a long time. While you are struggling through this, I am not. I don't consciously read. I glance at a word, and my brain knows it. I have read for years and years. I *cannot* be tricked here. I know that the word is not laughing. Try again."

So, sitting there with the coffee shop owners, I sadly had to explain that my industry lies. They *lie*—out-and-out, bald-faced lies. I know. I'm sorry. Not slight misrepresentations, but a real, honest to goodness lie. I told them that MC/Visa would not set up a business with no contract for any reason, and if they did, they wouldn't want the account. They invariably ask how I would know that, and it can be tempting to say, "I do this for a living," but that's not really what they're asking.

One has to grasp that if I say an industry is full of lies, at a bare minimum, one person is lying. Either it's that other guy or me. We both could be lying, but at least one of us is. I get that because, well, I do this for a living.

I asked if they would like proof.

Well, yeah, but that seems like a hard thing to do. I told them that my car (a black, glossy sportster just outside the townhouse window of their shop gleaming in the sun) would be on the line. I would bet that car against anything they had, such as the used granola bar wrapper they had on the table in front of me. Now, I had their attention. My car against a worthless wrapper. What could they lose?

"When this guy comes back, get him to tell you again that there is no contract. He will repeat it. 'No contract.' He'll confirm again because you're asking buyer questions. You're almost on the hook. Then tell him that you'll do it on the condition that he brings you no paperwork to sign and sends no emails to click 'approval.' He'll turn a very light gray. When he stammers and backpedals and says you must sign *something*, remind him there is no contract; he said so three times. This is a gentlemen's agreement; just bring your machine and set it up.

"He'll be on the edge of getting physically sick at that point.

"He'll explain his way out, but that there is a contract, and that what he probably meant was there was no term or time period to it (even then, there would have been if you didn't have him by the throat and point it all out). When all that ugliness is done, call me. I bring the paperwork, and you can give me my used wrapper."

They laughed but didn't really believe all that was going to happen. Two days later, I had a message that my car was safe (it was never in danger), and could they give me a different wrapper when I came out as they had thrown the other away?

13

ARE YOU COMPLIANT?

PCI compliance is a simple way of saying risk aversion in the industry. What kind of risk? Fraud. Fraud in my industry is what changes prices and burns up your profitability. Engrain this in your head:

The riskier the transaction, the higher the fee.

Simple right? PCI is a cover-your-buttocks theology adopted by the industry that you pay for, making it harder to sue them. Awesome!

It generally costs $5 to $10 a month as long as you're compliant. If you're not, it goes to $30 to $40. Stay compliant. This is done annually, but don't be surprised if you miss it. They love that. You'll pay the insurance to keep them safe. The real issue is that after a simple notice, everyone is fine with allowing your business—and millions of others—to pay the extra fee over and over, month after month. My firm simply adopted the policy to call all our customers right before the birthday of that business, which is getting set up. After all, that's when PCI compliance gets renewed. We call the business, tell them it's time for their PCI renewal (online), then walk them through it, and the customer is done in less than four minutes. How simple is that? It builds goodwill and saves our customers thousands of dollars.

It's called being a specialist. Do you really want to have to learn this every year? No, and I don't want to cut my grass. I have a guy who cuts, edges, and blows it down. My insurance guy (I love this one) has a staff member who calls and emails me and reminds me of all my important dates. Specialists. It's like a team of business commandos who, under the cover of night, infiltrate the enemy of all the things that eat my time and destroy them. That's what I want to do for clients as well. The last thing someone who just fixed their PCI non-compliance issue wants to do is fear this will happen again and that she'll miss it next year and start getting dinged again. Get rid of that.

14

THE GESTAPO IS COMING!

If you don't know what the Gestapo is, study some history. Nazis, people. Nazis. Unfortunately, this is a bad story. It's happened more than once, and it's happening right now somewhere.

A local business we support is a restaurant run by an Asian family who speak very broken English. They're the sweetest people, really, genuinely nice people. They love their adopted country and love the people—for the most part.

One evening, at about seven, the office phone rang. A full partner in the firm, Michael, answered the phone. He knew Tony, the husband in the business, well and responded to him with friendly surprise. Tony was surprised someone was there as it was late, but Michael had to come back to the office for something after a long meeting. He was fated to be there for Tony's call.

Tony (a name he adopted that was as close to his birth name as possible so Americans could speak it) was very nervous. A man was there.

"He say he an officer with the MC and the Visa. He say my machine is wrong and not compliant. That he will have to report me. He say that he can fix it if I sign his account." Mike listened and didn't know whether to laugh or utter a battle cry of anger. Tony had become a friend of his over the past few years, and Michael and his family had eaten at Tony's business many times. It was good.

"Is he still there?" Michael asked, fuming.

"Yes. Still here. Eating. He say he eat and give us time but have to know when he leave," Tony told him. Michael was seven minutes away. He got there in four. He would later say he wasn't sure if he remembered seeing lights or stop signs.

Michael knew the man upon entering the building. He had dealings with him before—all bad. The man looked up, saw Michael walking in, and turned very pale.

"Why, Doofus McGee, you look like someone just walked over your grave."

Doofus McGee is not the man's real name. Dear reader, you have no idea how I'd like to type his real name. There are Doofus McGees in every industry, making it harder for every honest person in that industry to do anything. They sow mistrust everywhere they go, thinking that this next score will make them so much they can retire, and it never happens.

Michael was doing his best Doc Holiday impression from the movie *Tombstone* as he relished this moment. But the best was yet to come. Doofus may or may not have spoken or said hello, but he was visibly sweating.

"Doofus, apparently, you are an MC/Visa *law officer*. Could you show me a badge?" Michael asked. Nothing. "Can you show me an email, text, or any communication, any piece of paper deputizing you to say what you're telling people?" Nothing. Doofus had stood up by this point and walked to the cash register. He wanted to pay. He wanted to leave. It was palpable. So, Michael continued, "I think you owe these people an apology."

"Sorry," Doofus squeaked out. It was utter humiliation. Michael would have felt sorry for this human, I guess, if he had not been so dastardly and tried to intimidate people and extort them into switching. The best was yet to come.

Doofus was up at the cash register. Tony, his wife, and Michael were all standing there. It was the definition of a walk of shame. Sheepishly, he pulled out his wallet. He never looked up. He never looked anyone in the eyes. He fumbled with it, pulled out his plastic, and handed it to Tony's wife. The next thing to happen will be a moment that will live in infamy in Michael's mind for the rest of his life. He tells this story to agents all the time about what people will do for money. He uses it to instruct and hopefully better their relationships with not just businesses but with the people who are the actual business. He teaches and retells it. At dinner parties and over drinks with the inner circle, he tells it to listeners who have heard it before and are still enraptured.

"Then, it happened," Michael tells people. "This guy was caught red-handed in a protection racket, standing there with his arm outstretched, handing Tony's wife his card for payment. Then, at that moment, she did something that made me want to kiss her on the mouth. I wanted to laugh out loud while drinking like we were Vikings in Valhalla. He had his arm out with his card in hand, and Tony's wife stopped him and said, "I'm sorry. We will need you to pay in cash."

As true as that is, as funny as it was, Tony later pulled Michael aside and told him he had never seen "a white guy turn *that* white."

15

THEY WILL COME FOR YOU

Tragically, that is not an isolated tale. A customer of mine, who has become a friend to me and shared many meals over long talks, called me to tell me about "a real Mensch." Just a really good guy who has a bed and breakfast downtown in Savannah's beautiful historic district. A visitor came in and told him he was "some kind of officer with MC and Visa." Seriously, this again? He told the man his system was woefully outdated and he would have to report him. He never said *exactly* what would happen, but he got the feeling that he was supposed to infer that he would be heavily fined or worse—like maybe it was a real crime and that the guy talking to him was a junior G-man. These higher-level people were getting a report, so whatever was wrong with his account wouldn't be lost in a fog; they would now have his exact data and whereabouts and were coming.

Yes, this happened.

I asked if his friend laughed in the guy's face. No, but he felt something was off. I called and met the man in person. I told him what a farce had been played out. I asked him a few questions, then flat out asked if it was a guy named so-and-so, as I suspected. Indeed, it was someone I had known and worked with. I was not surprised to see that he had gone to the dark side. No, it was not Doofus McGee from before.

There are no officers in the way these people describe. No, these two guys are a few steps away from running a protection racket. It was not Doofus from the restaurant, which makes it even worse. There's more than one of these guys right here in my hometown. They used the same ploy and somehow still slept at night. It's disgusting. I tell you this, dear reader, so that you know. I also say it just in case one of these shysters is reading this: You are human garbage, and I hope all this comes back to you. Honest money is good money. Put this behind you, and realize you make a better living, a better life, and better friends by putting into the system instead of ripping things out.

If someone like this comes to your business's doorstep, listen to them, get their card, name, and contact number, and take them very seriously. That part they will love. Then, tell them you'd like your lawyer, who works for Visa USA, to review your account and follow up with them to ensure their business is legitimate. They'll turn green. Take a picture. And please—pretty please, with sugar on top—send me a copy.

16

HOW YOU DO WHAT YOU DO

Aprocessor often wants to build a history with a client. This may seem weird, but keep in mind the risk principle we've discussed already. Even if you have been processing for years, a new processor may ask for things you think are silly because you've been around. Understand that processors do not share histories with one another. When they ask, it's a good thing. They're protecting themselves. They're also protecting you.

I was bringing a group aboard that had been processing for years. A company owned by a European group that did business in the US. They made fiberglass used in airplanes and police body armor and had many government contracts. It was a nightmare. Though it was all on their website, getting examples of what they did and sold was like trying to get access to Area 51 so you could look at the UFOs. Everything they sent was redacted with large black lines. You felt like it was an episode of the X-Files. It was a good account that ranged between $350 and $750 thousand a month. Little did I know—but I would later find out—their credit card processing was less than 1 percent of their sales. They were an actual player.

Even after jumping through more hoops than a circus tiger, we had to have them submit several invoices for some of their $60,000-a-piece orders for a while. They fussed a little at first, capitulated, and then the need for them disappeared. They were all good as far as the processor was concerned. It was just some due diligence. It makes sense. All you need to do to steal these days is very little. It's not a horse, mask, six-gun, or sack with a dollar symbol. You just need a merchant account and an internet connection.

How bad is it? Imagine you have a merchant account with no scruples whatsoever. None. You find a picture of a beautiful Mustang online and copy the picture. Then you get online, get on to eBay, and post the following:

For Sale: One Beloved Granddad's Mustang

As you can see, this is one beautiful car for $5,000. I can't keep it. I wanted this beauty my whole life. Now that my grandfather is gone, I can't bear to drive it. He'll never be in it with me. It's going for well under value. I just Want someone like me who's always wanted this Incredible car, but I could never afford one to get it.

If you want to know, almost that exact thing has happened before. It doesn't normally work, but when it does, *Wham!* Now, eBay Motors will put the money in escrow until the car is delivered with the title, but you'd be amazed at what has happened on other avenues. All you need to do is give them your credit card number.

17

FAR AND AWAY

I work with a lot of groups. I've worked with hospitals, charities, even the military. Specifically, I've had a PX in the Philippines and Japan. Those are odd calls to take. I'd have to be working at 7:00 p.m., so they could call me at their time or around 5:00 a.m. We preferred to work by email, as you can imagine. Most people in my industry will not get many chances to work across frontiers like that. I was able to skip-jack the issues, as the US Military is, well, the US.

Plus, and this was the real saving grace, they still had a US bank account that the money was going into. I can do that all day long with no effort. You can be deep in a Tibetan jungle, but if you are licensed as a US company and deposit to a US bank, MC/Visa says you might as well be on the corner down the street where Billy's dad got into that fender bender on his way to the community picnic where Aunt Martha is sure to win a blue ribbon for her Bread and Butter Pickles, just like every year.

18

LET THEM HEAR

I have given more than one talk to a group of college kids on university grounds. If I can get them before they go out and make every mistake in the world when they start a business, it'll be a little easier. A lot of what I cover in this book is in that talk, but I generally only get them for an hour max.

Traps, pitfalls, and other devices made to ensnare are the subject of the day. First, we talk about the effective rate. You're welcome. Then, we talk about machines being cheap and how there is always a contract—always. I know we've gone into that already, but that has caused more swearing than Loud Guy did that one time. Ask me how I know.

Then, as a natural progression, we speak about early termination fees. This is the piranha at the end of the rainbow. It is the left hand of the contract. It is the lock on the gate in the middle of the wall. It's what keeps you in and not moving to greener pastures. The early termination fee ensures you stay to the end of the contract's term until time is up.

Most contracts are three years, but there are longer, dirtier ones. Ask me how I know. Here's the thing: If there is no penalty for breaking loose early, who cares? So, they must have a penalty. Normally, this is $300 to $600. Normally. I am not crazy about those, but if they are going to be there, fine. Some contracts hit you for everything you're worth. Normally, when they get very down and dirty like that, it reads that if you leave early, you agree to pay the entire amount they would have earned from you over the rest of your term, plus legal fees. This can be $3,000 or more. Ask me how I know.

A nice pair of brothers from India ran a small liquor store. When the old owners sold it to them, they kept the same bank account, electric bills, and merchant account. Who cared? They still had the same bank account. It just kept depositing.

Okay, just for giggles, I'll tell you who cares: MC/Visa.

This is illegal. They are not on the account. It breaks the line of ownership of the transactions. If something happens, technically, the two brothers could walk away and say they have nothing to do with it. You must—must—have a re-signing of new owners at the change of ownership. A person can leave a business, but there must be new signings if the business is sold.

Now, as it happens, the brothers signed with us. When the old company asked them why they left, they checked a box on a form that said "better rates." They should have said, we bought this business and did not know we needed to resign as a new business owner and new merchant account. They hit the brothers with a $3,000 tab, which they said they would have gotten over the next couple of years. I had to step in and tell them they never had a contract with these brothers and that taking $3,000 from them was tantamount to fraud. I would be contacting MC/Visa USA on their behalf with legal representation. That changed the score. It also taught me two invaluable lessons early in my career:

1. Don't assume people know what they're doing.

2. A bank can go back up to sixty days and legally pull out any monies drafted out of an account, assuming it was electronically pulled out in the first place.

This brings up something that agents always ask, which we quickly incorporated into training. What if they're under contract? *Everyone* is under contract. If they are not, they don't have a merchant account. Don't believe me, go back and read where I bet my car. Everyone. Question number two then organically comes out of that (and organic is way healthier). Then, what do we do? We buy them out.

That assumes it is a reasonable amount. The two brothers above, though good men, had a business I would not buy out at $3,000, but those are rare, as it's a dirty pool. But they can be bought out, and when it's $300 to $600 per business, it's easy to make that business case. Many times, I don't have to. When the owner looks and sees they're a small business overpaying $2,400 a year, they just outright pay it themselves. It's clearly in their best interest.

Better yet, we show them how we don't do that. You see, we have a contract but no term. We say that up front as one should. If you're hiding something about your business, you might be the dirty pool player in the room. Don't do that. You're better than that. Besides, you've always been my favorite.

We tell people to challenge us when they sign up and say, "Show me my freedom. Where does it say I can leave at any time?" Gladly. As we sign for multiple processors, we have one of several things to show, but it normally comes down to one of two.

Either under term, it says "No term" or "0 years."

Or by early termination fee, it says "$0.00."

Notice the two places that are underlined. That's a slot where we can write or type something into. It's our choice. In either case, what we're doing is unlocking the gate. No term or a "0-year term" means you could leave tomorrow. By the same standard, I can sign someone to a 999-year term, like you're joining Scientology, but if I make it a $0 early termination fee, you could still leave whenever you wanted. MC/Visa will require you to leave your account open for thirty days while they close it out to make sure no chargebacks or refunds are pending and you can use it in the meantime to swipe cards, but other than that, you're in the wind.

I do that because I do what I say. If I have to lock you in, I probably won't be the best representative in the world. Our team is built on pay-for-performance. If we do the job, you'll be happy to be here. You shouldn't be obligated if we're not the right fit for you.

Many times in the industry, things are put to either hook you once you're in or to be waived to get you in. An example of this is an account I lost. Yes, yes, I know. You won't believe it. It's true. Early in my career at my own shingle, determined to be the best at what I do and the best for my customers, I blurted out such a truth that they never answered my call again. I use it as a teaching tool to this day.

19

THE LAST BOY SCOUT

I was in with a captain of industry here in Savannah. This guy was as big as a bull with a laugh just as big. He was no BS, quick on the uptake, and quick to decide. We chatted. I laid it out there and saved him money; it was going swimmingly. Don't worry; mistakes are coming.

"Will, I think we can move forward. This is a good fix, and I *do* like saving money. How much do I write the check for?" he bellowed. He was not trying to be loud; he was just big and blustery.

"Sir?" I asked. "There is no need to write a check. You need no equipment. We'll reprogram what you have."

"Yes, yes, I mean, how much do you need to make this happen?" he asked again.

"To get it all set up?"

Ah! It dawned on slowpoke me. Finally, the last horse crossed the finish line, and I mentally caught up. Those bogus fees people use in my industry are setup fees, paperwork fees, ratification fees, and renoberation (yes, this is a made-up word. No, I did not make it up. Comic strip artist Berkeley Breathed, of the comic strip *Bloom County,* used this nonsense word once when his character, instead of a monster, had two economists come out of his closet of anxieties. They used this word when arguing over the economy) of the Frankincense fee. Bunk. All Bogus. They have a hundred names, just like placebos come in a hundred styles and colors.

"Sir," I started in the most Boy Scout manner you have ever seen. I was going to wow this guy with honesty and integrity, then sit down and show him how to tie a sheepshank not to better serve God and country. "All those fees are not real. They're bogus. They only line the pockets of the reps who try to charge them to companies like yours. We don't do that type of thing. We would never charge you a bogus fee." I was sure that while I was speaking, somewhere behind me, an American flag took up the whole back of the room as it waved, and a bald eagle screeched its salute to my honesty. Eat your heart out, Patton.

There was something in the air, and it wasn't comradery. The man had grown imperceptibly colder, but it was different now. I had lost the room. I could never get him on the phone again, and no emails were answered. There was no one home.

Did you see it happen? Did you see where it all went wrong? If you did, you are quite astute or have made this mistake as well. I'm sorry. It's a hard lesson to learn, and I teach it to my agents and young salespeople now. Here's the breakdown. I called him an idiot.

Again, a few of you were shaking your heads earlier. Some were even softly squinting or clenching their teeth. That's because he was telling me what he expected. Not unlike me telling my insurance guy to drop the jargon, he was telling me—more than once—that he had, in fact, paid that fee at least once in the past. My response (in his mind) told him that *he was a dummy, and I knew it, as he had confessed he had paid these "bogus fees to line the pockets of the reps."*

Was I ever so young?

How do I fix this? The training is specific. When someone asks what my setup fee is—or insert the name of the bogus fee you have heard of—here's how it is answered: "Sir, I see what you are trying to do. Really, you don't know me from Adam. Am I a person, and is my company the type who would try to get you to pay one of these bogus fees? No. My company gladly doesn't even have them to be offered because you and I *both* know the moment I said, 'Now, just pay me this bogus fee," you'd tell me to high tail it out of here. So, did I pass your test?"

This works. Ask me how I know.

Sadly, there are many of these fees. None are real. They had legitimate roots in the mid-eighties, as we were still building the infrastructure. Seriously, that didn't come about overnight. Now, it's as real as a unicorn or a whale.

By that, I mean it's used in a high-pressure close. Man, how I hate those. Please dump the high-pressure close. I stop people in it. It's just not necessary. In merchant accounts, though, there are companies that put a whole slew of these official-looking fees in with little boxes next to them. Then, the person comes in, does all this dog-and-pony show, and asks for the close.

They get a pushback. That's when the real dance begins. They say, "What if I can scratch off some of these? What if I can get them waived?" You should start hearing the music from *Jaws*. They'll then go into an explanation that is as rich as it is untrue. If you were ready to sign today, they would be willing to go to bat for you. They could call their manager and ask—and really push for—these things to get a partial wave. But they only have so many times they can push for that, well, you understand. If the customer isn't ready, they can return another day. *But* if the customer was ready to go today—as long as some of those were wiped out or reduced—then they would make that call. They just can't make that call if you, as the customer, aren't really serious. They can't get that egg on their face with the boss.

That guy is a rep-eater. He's good at his job, mind you, but serious. He has too many big clients. What's that? You mean you'd sign today *if* I could waive all these absolutely bogus charges and fees? Gee-willickers, mister. I don't know. I know these are all fake, but if you're ready to sign, like right now, I'll make that call. Can I go outside? It might get loud. I need to pace a little while you watch me from a distance. I have to check my voicemail and pretend it's my boss chewing me out for giving in to a customer. Don't worry; I'll be waving my hands to imitate like you're ready right now, and this is the only holdback.

Hey, guess what? I have partial hearing damage from my fake boss's call, but he agreed to waive the fees. Yes, all of them, as you are signing today.

There's a second insidious reason to have those fees on there: the whale. Now, the whale is not always as big of a client as you might think. No, it's just someone, often a small to middle client, who doesn't know to try and kick out of the deal to get it sweetened. No, they are looking at all the stuff, swamped in all the numbers. They are unsure, as this is their first foray into all of this, or they have one, which is really costing them. They need this, and they know it. They should know that they have a hundred options, but they feel you know what you're doing—and they kind of need this.

Reps love these whales because they will get a whale of a commission. This is because, just like I explained to that captain of industry, it goes right into their pockets. I have seen people get popped for $900 in start-up fees. Nine hundred dollars! For things that were free and had no cost to the agent or the firm setting up the account. Let me explain the insanity behind this if you think this is a sweet deal for the agent. This is, in fact, a time bomb waiting to go off. Just like me, someone will end up saying (hopefully more tactfully than my green-horn wording did earlier) that all those are not real fees. This will happen.

When it does happen, what does that client think of that rep? They think that they were willing to take big advantage of them for a few bucks and that they are just flat-out crooks, and they would be right. There is nothing worth your good name in your field or any other. It will follow you.

While waiting tables back in school, it was a big no-no to double-tag someone. Double tagging is when a tip is added automatically because of the size of the table, but you give them their receipt in such a way (not pointing out that a tip has been added already) that they add a (second) tip. Well, one fine day, which was actually early evening, there was a table of eight people, so the tip was added automatically. They were very sweet and nice to deal with, but afterward, an older woman left extra cash on the table—not a lot, but $2. Realizing they had already tipped me, I ran after her. She was in the parking lot and was slightly startled that this young man came charging out like the building was on fire. I thanked her, apologized for the startle, and explained that their tip had been added already. As she wasn't the cardholder, she probably didn't realize that she didn't need to kick anything in. She laughed and told me she knew all that but was leaving a little extra anyway, as I had been very attentive. Even at $2, that compliment was worth much more to my heart. Even better was that about a year later, there were some questions at a table about the bill. By then, I was managing. I came up and was answering the question when this lady popped her head in from the others and said words that cannot be bought:

"Bill, it's correct. This is Will. He's waited on me in the past. He once chased me into the parking lot because he feared I overpaid by $2. If he says it's right, it's right."

Thank you, ma'am.

20
CAPITALISM AT ITS BEST

I'll tell you what I love. I love a great story about capitalism. A businessperson, man or woman, who succeeds despite some daunting obstacles through sheer force of will and creativity. I love it because it's always endearing. As human beings, we like the art of creation. Why do you think so many shows and movies have the ubiquitous hard-work scene? You know the one. The movie is two-thirds over, and they have to knuckle down and do all the work while a major song from the soundtrack plays, creating a montage. Rocky is really getting into his training. The kids from opposing backgrounds are learning to get along, or the dysfunctional team is learning to mesh together as they build the big thing in the movie.

This is so innate in us as human beings; we describe things around us as positive when that may sound odd. Driving by an old Victorian home that has a few fresh pine boards unpainted on its side is nice to see. Some people like the whir and sounds of a dishwasher or clothes turning in a dryer with a front window. This is because they are all work, and work means life. If you disagree, riddle me this: Why do people buy ant farms?

I like the story of Nathan's Hotdogs, which includes true business zeal. Nathan worked at a restaurant that sold hotdogs for ten cents each. Nathan Handwerker, a Polish immigrant, thought he could do better. He saved money, as supposedly he could eat for free there. Using his grandmother's recipe with his wife's help and a loan from two friends, he struck out on his own.

He had a big issue, though.

Hotdogs are not expensive fare. Eating them in 1916 for ten cents was one thing, but he had to undercut the competition. He had to beat them at the game and go for the longer sale and not the quicker buck. So, he charged a nickel for his. Now, inexpensive food is food that will sell, but selling them for what was considered almost nothing made people doubt them. Were they safe? What was in these things that he could even do that? They couldn't be safe, could they?

Again, this is where the entrepreneur Nathan came in. Doctors, he needed doctors, but where to get them? He hired them—kind of. He hired men in white coats to stand around at the lunch rush and eat his hot dogs. He never *said* they were doctors, and if people thought a bunch of doctors were always at Nathan's, Nathan couldn't stop them. People think what they want.

It worked like gangbusters. People started buying his dogs. The more that bought, the more people walking by thought that those guys must know something they didn't. So, they bought them, too. The bandwagon was jumped on and hard by hungry people who wanted an inexpensive lunch. Then, the Fourth of July rolled around, and things would never be the same. Because Nathan Handwerker was Polish and an immigrant, he deeply loved his adopted country. He loved its opportunities and its embracing of him and his family.

As people are bound to do, Nathan and three other immigrants who also loved their new country argued over who loved her the most. Remember what I said about boys and the game King of the Hill? This is what we do.

So, they were trying to decide which immigrant (all from differing lands) loved America the most. Nathan finally said a hot dog eating contest should decide it. The winner, an Irish immigrant, ate twelve hot dogs. Today, Nathan's annual hot dog eating contest draws as many as one million viewers on ESPN, and sixty thousand show up in person. Nathan has become the institution.

I get to see this every day. Really. Men and women business owners who bust up all odds to make something special. I know restauranteurs that people drive an hour to eat at. I know bed and breakfasts with families coming back year after year, sometimes booking twelve months prior, and blue-collar craftsmen with white-collar companies begging at their doorsteps to take them on for work.

One local woman, a master of fusion, had a special wood-fired pizza oven modified with a special trailer to take it to pop-up events. You have never had pizza like this. The first time my wife tried it (on the first bite), she exclaimed, "Oh! It's like a song in my mouth!" Her pizzas all have wild and fresh ingredients, and one even has potato slices. Don't knock. It may sound like carb overload, but I've had it, and it's incredible. This same woman made a fusion of kimchee cream cheese and woodfired bagels that are the delight of the whole town. You can't make that up.

Yet, many of these businesses use pay-as-you-go accounts like Stripe, Square, and even PayPal. They have no idea until shown how much of their hard-earned business dollars are rolling out the doors. Understand a pay-as-you-go account has its place—a well-earned place. That place is in the rare-use service and for the people who would spend $10 on a box of Cheerios when you and I wouldn't pay more than $3.50.

It gets hot here in the Deep South. Savannah is right on the coast. I grew up smelling saltwater. It's a God given gift that I understand not having. That being said, it comes with mosquitoes that you can throw a saddle on and so much humidity that in late July and August, we develop gills to help us breathe. My maternal grandfather is one of those people who they told to move out to Arizona in the early sixties so the dry air would help his emphysema. Here, the air would end up shortening his life. It can get seriously thick.

For winters that people up North describe as being "mild air conditioning," we often have gas heat in our homes. Let me tell you, it's not used a lot. So, we have months on end that the gas, unless it's what your stove runs on, is never used and not even thought about. Come down South for a spell, and you will be introduced to cool side dishes—tomatoes, cucumbers, corn salads, all kinds of things to help you cool off. Way off. What we don't need is that gas heat.

But we have to pay for it anyway.

Every month, there is a fee of $30 to $40 for not using gas—*not* using it. Does this make sense? We don't use it. We never turn it on. This is hard to oversell. If I turned on my heat right now in late July as I write with a glass of well-iced tea, my house and the four houses nearest me would burst into flames, and multiple magnolia trees would lose their pungent blossoms as they wailed in pain. All the while, I am still paying for that gas bill.

This is a worthy idea for pay-as-you-go accounts to opt to counter. They went after the people on the sidelines and fringes—all the small shops and boot-strappers working every swap meet they could hit. Businesses that might get one or two cards a week, or maybe even several on Saturday, and then nothing for a month and a half. Those guys have often felt pushed out of the merchant account world because they haven't built up enough need to take plastic, but in the meantime, they were turning clients away because they couldn't. Then, the pay-as-you-go account pops onto the scene. Now, they have an option—a real, viable option.

Because it's all the little ancillary fees, all the ankle-biters eat them up because they haven't grown to that point yet. The gas bill in August fee. They can't do the small stuff that would eat up all the profits from when they do. So, what do they do? They get a pay-as-you-go account.

Pay-as-you-go accounts charge once for a transaction. If you run a transaction today and nothing for two months, you only pay on today's transaction. That is good news. That is great news, in fact. It says that you now have the key to the executive bathroom and access to its privileges. Namely this: No turning away clients. The people rejoice. Huzzah!

So, why do I not like these types of accounts? Actually, I do. They are great launch pads to get into markets and get business that you might normally have to pass on. Trust me, I have seen every type of thing you can imagine. One was a business that was processing his friend's credit card sales. So, here is my question: As a professional, have you ever seen something done that induced nausea so bad that you felt like you turned the color gray? I felt that when I couldn't explain quickly enough to a seemingly non-insane business owner. I understood why he did what he did. I am sure his friend was not a bad guy. Did he understand that MC/Visa would de-list him immediately if they found that out? What was the likelihood of that? Well, for one, when one of these people called and performed a chargeback saying they had not spent that money at his place of business, he could either A) decide to eat the loss and shut way, way up, or B) he could tell them that he was illegally exposing the system to multiple layers of fraud and get himself de-listed for his confession.

I've seen everything, including the above, and prefer the pay-as-you-go account. I had side businesses back in the day and would have loved a pay-as-you-go account. Where it doesn't help is once a business has grown into a steady flow of cards. It's one thing to do less than $1,000 a month, or even every two months, but when you're doing $2,000, $5,000, or $20,000 a month and using a pay-as-you-go account, you're probably hemorrhaging.

I explained this to a woman who was a *big* believer in the little white-squared device. Oh, how she would sing its praises. Then, as she was there for an education, she looked at me and said, "Oh, you have *variable* rates?" If you could have seen the look she gave—the inflection in her voice. It was a pejorative. It was almost disgust and probably was, as she had found out, like Loud Guy, that I was a crook stealing people's hard-earned money. I probably kicked puppies and told kids there was no Santa for fun.

That's when I asked her if she liked variable-rate restaurants.

I love food—love it. I often come back to it to use as an example, so bear with me. We'll grab lunch later. Seriously, though, variable-rate restaurants. Did she like them? What did I mean? Well, what I mean is when I go out to eat, I want to eat in a variable-rate restaurant, not a one-rate restaurant. At a one-rate place, you go in and ask how much the lobster is—the big one. It's $32. Hmmm, maybe that's a little steep for a Wednesday. How much is the steak? It's $32. Okay, I am ordering in the highbrow area. What about a burger? $32. Tuna salad? $32. A side order of fries? $32. A complimentary glass of water? $32.

The Dollar Store works when it's $1. It stops working if everything is $54. Who goes into an "Everything Under $300" store? Not me. But that is what you're getting.

III

How Much is Taken Out?

1

WHAT IT REALLY COSTS

Let's put this down to apples to apples. A pay-as-you-go account for a retail organization is normally 2.75 percent. Credit card? 2.75 percent. Debit card? Rewards card? 2.75 percent. Does that sound good?

A standard merchant account for a business will put a credit card transaction at between 1.60 and 1.70 percent. A debit card is a safer transaction (riskier is more expensive, thus safer is less expensive) because it's not based on your good name but on a finite amount of money you have in the bank at that exact moment. Therefore, it is about half that at 0.89 percent. A rewards card is the most expensive (your business pays that card's sky miles, bon voyage) and comes to 1.99 to 2.4 percent.

If you think you were never that good at math, I'm here to help. *All of those are less than 2.75 percent, and most by far.*

Don't feel bad. I'm a slow reader. I know it. It takes me forever to read a book, especially if I read in bed for five whole minutes before slipping into this mortal coil. If you need a test to know if you're a slow reader, this is the test. When you go to a movie and words come on screen at the beginning of the movie explaining part of what's going on, do you panic?

Being bad at math is different. You're probably thinking that because you couldn't find the tangent of the angle you were looking for in the few minutes you had in sixth-grade math on that one test, you're not good at math. Humbug! I've known more people who "weren't good at math" who could split a bill at the restaurant five ways and calculate in their head which bottle of cleaner at the store was the best buy in cost per ounce, and that was before they started putting that on the labels. Most people are decent at math. However, this industry takes advantage of the situation and makes it more complex than it is.

This is not Advanced Algebra, Trigonometry, Calculus 3.0, or anything that you need a third-level wizard with a bag of moonstones to be able to conquer. Congratulations if you know that one is less than two, and two is less than three. You can do this—easily. Every game in the book is put to play to keep you from the information. This is for an important reason. You're not dumb, and you're not that bad at math. If you had all the data and none of the filler these use to create these things from simple reports into cumbersome boilerplate, you could probably figure it out.

You've seen how they'll show you your numbers without going into a percentage to make your brain think you have a percentage like Loud Guy's 0.03125. Even then, if he had taken just a moment, he would have known that $600 is more than 1 percent of $20,000. The thing is that the numbers are put there for you to lean and rely on. *Well, I guess this is my rate. Hmmm, you know, that seems like a good rate.*

On a side note, let me say this: If you are paying one-third of 1 percent and are looking to have your rate lowered, you might be greedy. Also, remove the words "might be" from that last sentence and exchange them with "are."

Don't trust these numbers with blank stares. There is a reason we have the phrase, "Keep an honest man honest."

"Trust but verify" also works. A little homework and some side work, and most of this will make sense.

Here is a second way that pay-as-you-go accounts will spank you. They get to break a hard and fast rule in the industry. That rule is that you *must* show in your report the different card types used *because* you have to show that business what they were charged on each card type. That is what lets them violate this inviolate rule. Right now, you're thinking, *Will, that doesn't make a lick of sense.*

Bear with me, Grasshopper.

The last time, and just for giggles, I looked at the list of reward cards for MC and Visa was a couple of years ago. I have to know that they're there. It doesn't aid me in my day to day to study the list. That'd be like a car mechanic memorizing the hundreds of tires he could put on a car. I will say this, though: It was large. Visa had about twenty-five pages of rewards cards listed in small print, single-spaced. They were not trying to eat up pages but to fit more on. It was page after page of cards. We'll get into that in a bit, but we have this rabbit trail to follow first. MC made that look like a bunch of rank amateurs with 118 pages of rewards cards. *One hundred and eighteen pages.* Single-spaced, tightly knit together. Pages. Pages and pages. One hundred and eighteen. Dear reader, understand the number of contracts, documents, phone calls, handshakes, and bartering that took. It's incredible.

The ancient city of Alexandria is known for two things. The first is the Lighthouse of Alexandria. At 350 feet tall, it was the largest thing in the ancient world, second only to the Pyramid of Giza. Its impressive stature made it a wonder to behold, and it is listed as one of the Seven Wonders of the Ancient World. I'm sorry to say that the Library of Alexandria shames it. The library, though not one of the Seven Wonders, is the great leap forward in my mind.

As a major port, shipping came there from all over the known world—and sometimes unknown. Well, the Alexandrians had a habit instilled by their government. They would board the ship and demand its book—all of them, and by force if necessary. They would then copy the books and return them unharmed. This became a type of shipping tax, and as they were always returned, it never impeded any shipping. But what did it accomplish? It made them the Google of the ancient world. They were the fount of knowledge—disparate knowledge, as different ideas from different lands and sources came pouring in. It opened new ways of thinking and different views on the challenges they faced. It single-handedly helped the ancient world lurch forward in a giant mental convulsive leap, trying to get up a good head of steam. The world moved.

That is what I think of every time I remember that MC had 118 pages of rewards cards. It would take a library to hold all the documents, papers, decisions, and signings made to go into that.

Now, that doesn't mean that every time you get a statement at your business, you have to be provided with all card types and all rewards cards that MC and Visa have, respectively. They only have to list what cards a business took in and how much was charged for each one. So, how might one get around that if one wanted to? Well, let's imagine we had a restaurant that, oh, I don't know, only had one price. I wouldn't have to formally list that you had lobster, a side order of fries, and a complimentary glass of water with all their separate prices listed, would I? No, all I would have to do is list that you had one item (the lobster), one item (the side order of fries), and one item (the complimentary glass of water). Everything is $32 each. So, your bill would look like this at the old One Rate Restaurant:

3 items at \$32: \$96
+ auth fees

In other words, you don't have to break down the card types *if* you have one rate because the breakout shows the rate you pay on each card. So, at the One Rate Restaurant, instead of your bill stating you had lobster, fries, and water with their individual prices, it just has to show how many things you ordered. The prices are a known entity.

I hate this. Hate, hate, hate.

In the first quarter of accounting (Yes, that story. Yes, I know quarter as opposed to semester means I'm old. No, I'm not an accountant.), they taught us in the first week—and probably on the first day—"If you have two businesses, you want two sets of books." Everyone groaned. Two? No one really wanted to be in that class. They didn't want to become accountants and certainly didn't want to be accountants times two. Why two sets of books? Isn't that needlessly complicated?

"Well," she said, "Imagine you have a gas station and a floral shop." I guess she was going for radically different to help us mentally separate them. "And you have one set of books, and you're making \$25,000 in monthly profit. Congratulations, you're a success. That's a pretty good living. But then, an accountant comes in and, just for giggles, creates two sets of books: one for each individual company. That's when you find out that your floral shop is making \$35,000 a month in profit and your gas station is costing you \$10,000 a month. Your job is to go murder the gas station right now. One business, half the headaches, and more profit with just the floral shop. But you'd never know that without *two sets of books.*"

Everyone in the class sat upright—all of us. She had our full attention. This wasn't her first rodeo. She had done more business's books, caught more people stealing companies blind via forensic accounting, and taught more classes of bored college kids who just wanted to please be set free so they could go ahead and take over the world. I think she actually said this all in the first hour of the first class. She was good—damn good.

I always think of this when I see white statements for these types of accounts. A business needs to see what type of business they are really in. The cards might as well be tarot cards in a gypsy's hands because, boy, they tell the tale. Without knowing them, you're like a business owner with one set of books for two companies. You're flying blind.

2

SINGLE MALT ONLY, PLEASE

I do not drink a lot, but I do drink. Since I am Scottish by heritage, I will drink Scotch. I don't drink blended Scotch. It makes me shudder, and not in a good way. Single malt only. In the process of making this stuff, they can keep it pure and keep the Scotch from a barrel in a single barrel, or they can blend several together.

No, thank you. I think this is a trick.

Japanese Sake or rice wine should not be served warm like James Bond and so many others told you. It's a trick. Warmed Sake was a trick done by lower-end restaurants to mask the flavor of poorer-quality Sake. Real Sake, the good stuff, is not warmed. Now you know. I do not know this to be true for blended, but it makes me shudder. I suspect it's an issue to sand down the rough edges. Blend it all together. No, thank you. Single malt, please.

Why that story? So, I can say that I don't like blended Scotch, and I don't like blended rates. See what I did there? A blended rate might as well be a blank on the rate. You don't know. You'll be flying blind.

A great example of this is the liquor store owned by the two brothers. Yes, there was another issue, but we can learn from it. The issue is that they had a blended rate. They did about

$15,000 a month in plastic under the one banner of a blended rate. My friends, this is the same as two businesses and one set of books. Oh, what we did on their books was amazing. It was such a deep dive that Indiana Jones was amazed at the adventures we had—digging old bones, treasure, a cursed tomb. You're not buying it, are you?

Okay, there was no cursed tomb. Also, though there would be digging later, we did this in about forty-five seconds once we looked at a statement. Did the statement say *blended rate* up in big, bold letters at the top? Of course not. And X never, ever marks the spot. But we did quickly look at a statement for the previous month and saw that they had done a solid $15,000 in sales and were paying about 1.60 percent as a discount rate for a standard credit card. Okay, great. They're doing pretty good. So, look down, a little farther down, almost there... got it: debit cards. Well, with 1.60 percent, their debit card rate should be pretty low, right? Actually, it was 1.60 percent. They had a blended rate. Do you see? It was blended into one number to make one homogenous whole of 1.60 percent.

But it doesn't really. I can paint a house to look like a car, but I can't drive it to Atlanta. So, the next thing to do once we see a blended rate—because we know that when we hear someone yell "Yeehaw," the next sound will be a crash—is to call 911. We know what's next. We look at the dollar amount in sales for credit cards and the dollar amount in sales for debit cards. Out of $15,000, more than $11,000 was in debit cards, and a little over $3,000 was in credit cards. Three Card Monty strikes again!

They were paying a good rate on those credit cards and had been lured in, but the bulk of their transactions were debit cards. Credit cards were only 20 percent of their sales, but they had a good rate on them. I think that is worthy enough to overlook a little thing like overpaying double what you should be paying on 80 percent of your transactions, right?

I mean, what's twice the cost on four out of five cards that come in between friends?

The worst thing is having to explain this to people. Most people want to believe that the guys they deal with are on the up-and-up. "Trust but verify," in this case, would have saved thousands of dollars a year. Sadly, I have to tell these people that they have been overcharged, and this other group knows better. They can see you did almost all debit cards. The issue is that while you tell people they have been dealing with snake oil salesmen, it makes you look like you also might deal in the oil of serpents.

That's when you show them how to do the effective rate calculation. It puts the power back into their hands. They get to see that and put it in effect every month or so to keep you honest.

3

THE ROMANTIC INNS
ASSOCIATION

Doesn't that just conjure up images? I live here, and it moves me. They are more expensive, but a bed and breakfast in a historic home in Savannah, Georgia, beats the Holiday Inn anytime—hands down, game over.

The first time I met Thom, I was sitting in the front sitting room of a Victorian home here in Savannah called *the Catherine Ward House-Inn*. The architecture, the art, and the colors all went together like a mosaic. He even had a little brass piglet sleeping on a miniature stool over on the corner from the sitting area. How I covet that pig and stool is hard to explain. They add such a unique flare to a beautiful home. Thom and I became friends, and I stayed there for my honeymoon. Thom had a bottle of champagne for me, and the newly minted Mrs. Black was waiting for us. It was a seal on one of the most wonderful nights of our lives, and rightly so.

But that first time sitting in his parlor was a sight to behold. You have to drink it in. It's wonderful. As we sat and chatted about what we did and how we did it, he listened, commented, and moved forward with us that afternoon. We were off to the races. Little did we know the quagmire we'd all be in less than sixty days later. Spoiler alert: It all works out. I wouldn't be married for a while yet.

So, we get his numbers, take them back to Santa's workshop, find the red ink, and submit them to him. Thom would save a little under $2,000 a year in fees. Awesome. Let's do it. This is right at the edge of the 2008 recession. A month later, he would be in season, which is like the lunch rush for a restaurant. It was his high point of the year. He got his first statement from us, and *wham!* He was paying more—a lot more.

Now, I know what I am doing. I did not lie to this man, nor did he think we lied to him. But he had an issue. Money was flowing out. What happened? This was a phone call, and it was pleasant, but I still had an issue. I am a professional, and I take this to heart. I don't do something good for me but bad for a client—ever. There are other accounts.

My mind was racing, and an image formed in my head. I told him I suspected what had happened but didn't want to oversell it. Could he please send me that recent statement and let me review it firsthand? Of course. It was on its way. I told him not to worry and that it didn't matter that he was in a contract, and we would make it work no matter what. If it wasn't good for him, it wasn't good for us. This guy and his business became a team effort. I can honestly say that no one here at the time did not review this with me. It was *all hands on deck*. It was not a huge account. It wasn't even in the top half, but my reputation was on the line. This would not do. We were going to find the issue, correct it, and make it a win for this guy if we made no money whatsoever. We told him it would be a savings, and we made sure it would be.

We would end up getting another statement from his files from the same time the previous year. I was right. It was the end of the beginning of the recession. It's a hard time to explain if you weren't in it. The short answer is people were scared.

They weren't pushing the gas; they were pushing the brakes. It was big; it was sudden, and no virus was involved. People and businesses were scared. Companies were downsizing. Does any of this sound familiar to those either not alive then or not old enough but seeing things now in 2020?

I am no Sherlock Holmes, though I do love a good Basil Rathbone as the detective, and I think he has the coolest name in history. Still, my investment of time and energy in the field I worked in and my sober reflections on what was happening in the country's financial concerns paid off in about fifteen seconds. I just had to and did confirm what I thought all along. It was the rewards cards. They were there and eating him alive.

A rewards card is a specific beast. It's made to incentivize people to spend. To get into that, we would need to talk about cognitive dissonance. That is a fancy way of saying that if you smoke cigarettes and know that they are bad for you, you say it was a bad day, so you deserve it, or it's okay to have one. Boom. Cognitive dissonance. If you think I'm scolding smokers, hold on. I could do it with smoking, overeating, or anything.

We as a nation love to spend. We are wealthy as a nation and love to get the money out of our pockets. Now, we can get money out of our pockets that we haven't even gotten yet with a credit card. I could go on and tell you that most first-world nations pulled themselves out of the mire via credit. That's another conversation, but it's amazing. It's good. But anything can be abused. If you know you shouldn't spend the money but go ahead and put it on the card, you have an issue. Talk to your mom.

Rewards cards tell us that spending gets us more than what we were simply buying. We'll get sky miles. We'll get points. We'll get free hugs, overnight stays in their hotels, upgrades, and who knows what. Back in the schoolyard, other kids would say, "If you give me one of your Nutter Butter cookies, I'll be your best friend." That often seems to have more sustenance and substance than these promises. Do you think it's hard to read a merchant statement? You'd have to follow and track most of this data in such a way that makes the CIA Counterintelligence team look like a bunch of yokels. But it tells the customer, "Go ahead and eat out at the place you can't afford again. You're getting sky miles!" Awesome, because I will need to fly far away once my credit is destroyed.

I am not saying everyone destroys their credit and that you can't take advantage of these things decently or responsibly. But I do know who pays the bulk—the lion's share, as they say in poetic language—for those sky miles, and it's not the airline.

It's also not the card issuer.

It's the business. True story. Look it up. In all the articles I've written for blogs, posts, and business periodicals, I've written most often and most voluminously on rewards cards as damage to the business where they are used. A rewards card can almost double the cost of a normal credit card and all but triple a debit card's rates. How? Is it riskier? Harder to verify?

I'll never forget about the best line from Will Smith's movie *Independence Day*. The president and all these survivors, basically refugees, go to the fabled Area 51, where all the conspiracy theorists say the government has hidden UFOs, and in the movie, they were right. They had been hiding them. When the president asks where they got all the funding for this, the father of the genius in the room says, "Well, you don't think a hammer costs $600, do you?" mocking the extreme spending in some military contracts that had been in the news.

Hammers do not cost $600. You might spend that much on a hammer, but it's not worth it—nor is a rewards card riskier and thus more expensive. It's more expensive because there is another business partner in the board room all of a sudden, and he gets a percentage. Guess who's paying the bulk of it? When a person comes into a business and pulls out a rewards card, what does it cost the business? Let's put that in perspective.

You own a store that makes fine furniture. One of your popular items is a $400 chocolate brown leather ottoman. Its buttery smooth texture makes people hear angels sing when they kick off their shoes at the end of a long day and throw their tired dogs up on its back. "The day is over," it says. "Relax."

A customer walks in, says they want that ottoman, and pulls out a credit card. What does that cost your business? If you have a good rate, it will be about 1.61 percent and $0.18 per transaction—not bad. A person sees them buying that and wants one as well. They pull out their debit card. What does that cost? Again, at the time of this writing and assuming you have a decent rate, it's about half of the prior, as it's a substantially safer transaction. It should be about 0.89 percent and $0.25 per transaction—not bad. Not bad, indeed. A final customer sees all these luscious chocolate brown ottomans going out the door and thinks they will not be left in the dark. They want to get one, too. You start thinking to yourself that if it continues like this, you're going to rename your store the Ottoman Empire (and the drummer beats out a rim shot).

So, he grabs one, goes to the counter, and pulls out his rewards card. This is where ominous music would start playing in a movie—the theme from *Jaws* or "The Imperial March" from *Star Wars*, which sounds an awful lot like "Mars, Bringer of War" from Holst's *The Planets*. I think John Williams was a Holst fan. Anyway, he pulls out his rewards card. How much does it cost your business?

Probably about 2.4 to 2.6 percent and $0.35 per transaction. You just went up about 60 percent in fees. Why—because it was a riskier card? Nope. You have a new business partner involved. Skyjam Airlines made a deal and got a card issuer to pull out a rewards card that gets your third client two sky miles every time he spends $3 million on their card in a sixty-day period. But Skyjam isn't pulling their weight, and neither is the card issuer nor is MC or Visa, depending on who is on the card. No, the bulk of the fees are paid by your business. To put this in perspective:

- The customer gets the ottoman and the sky miles.

- Skyjam gets the glory for giving away all these sky miles.

- Your business paid for most of it.

- Sign me up!

So, here is what happened to this poor bed and breakfast.

The recession had kicked in. Really, it kicked a lot of businesses and people who relied on the businesses in that economy for jobs and the economy itself in the teeth. The end of the beginning was here. People had gotten used to it. The big panics were over. It had already happened if someone got downsized, fired, let go, or reduced in pay instead of let go. Now, many people who were better off than most and hadn't been fired and could still stay at a $300-a-night bed and breakfast were still booking rooms. But they did something totally different than they had in the past because it was now a different landscape in the economy.

Rewards cards had been around for a bit, and all these people had them. They used a little cognitive dissonance and said to themselves that the worst was through; they could still go on vacation and to bed and breakfasts as they used to; they just might not be so extravagant. Also, they would put it on their rewards card. That would be a responsible thing to do, right? It didn't hurt anyone after all, and it was kind of like having a double-coupon day at the store. They'd go on vacation, but they would *do it all on a rewards card* and at least get points, sky miles, and virtual hugs, and of course, the Skyjam corporation would be their best friend.

Okay, I'm done barfing. I suspected that was what happened. I asked for and got the statement for the same month from the previous year. It set all my thoughts in stone as we read it and saw that this year, the bed and breakfast had taken in over *four times* the number of rewards cards that they had taken in their biggest month the year before.

This is a pain, but it's also your chance to shine. Don't be the ocean of nameless faces. Take responsibility. Speak. Fix it. Pretend that the customer is your best friend. You want the best for your best friend.

I called Thom and explained what happened. He was a bit down, but he understood. That's when I told him the good news.

"What's the good news?" he asked.

"The good news, Thom, is that you didn't sign a contract like with other guys where you suddenly become important to me when your contract is about to expire. You signed up with a firm that said we would help you with your account. We'll fix this even in the face of these changes, so this is a net win for you—not a kind of win, but a win."

That's when we made changes to his account to ensure it would decapitate all the big spikes he saw. It basically leveled out all the rewards cards and took not all the damages but the real brunt of them. He was pleased, but I could tell he would still be anxious to see his numbers next month when the new statements came out.

That time rolled around as it always did, and he called me and told me it was much better and that he was happy he was with me and my firm. That's when I told him about the good news.

"What's the good news?" he asked me over lunch.

"The good news is that you're with us," I told him.

"Yes. I know that. Thank you for fixing the issue," he said.

"No, no. You don't understand," I told him. "It's not that I could fix this, but that you weren't still with the other group."

"How do you mean?"

"I mean that we set your account up the exact same way as before since it has always worked for you. We just saved you the money they were overcharging all this time," I went on.

"And?" he asked.

"And imagine if you were still with them. You'd have lost the overcharges you were already being overcharged, *and* you would have been shredded when all these rewards cards rolled around. I hear every day from businesses that they are only important to their provider when they are about to sign up and when they are about to leave. Some have been told flat out, 'Your contract doesn't end until…' and then they know they're really stuck."

"Will," he said and stopped eating. He looked me right in the eyes. "You told me it didn't matter about a contract or not. If it wasn't good for me and my business, it wasn't good for you. I had no doubt at that moment. Trust me. You have a client for life."

That was a good day for us, and it showed us a sea-change type shift in their industry. We were able to speak to many more clients, all with unique and beautiful landmark homes, to help them solve their issues as well. This case, though, was ultimately two-fold. Yes, the explosion of rewards cards was something that had not happened before and hasn't been as big of a deal in the past few years. It was big then, and that was what counted. The other was that so many people with businesses were all but told, "You're in a contract" or, "Your contract doesn't end until…" which is the same as saying, "We'd care if we were trying to get you to sign'" or, "We'd care if we were about to lose you." That is no way to run a business with clients who have an issue, and it is no way to run your business if you're only important to your providers every three years.

4

THE OLD LADY AND THE
LEASE... FINALLY

I know we've already talked about leases, but this is a good time to bring up a specific case. There was once an old lady who lived in a, well, she lived at home but was the owner of a western wear shop. A shop that was closed—closed for good.

The recession was still on, and it was mid-2009. Again, many businesses that were on the edge closed with the downturn of income. This western wear shop had been one of them. I don't know if she bought it from other owners or if it had always been hers, but I do know that she was in trouble. She was in trouble, as she had closed the business, was living on a fixed income, and was well into the autumn of her life. Her exact age escapes me, but she was either in her late eighties or nineties. I know this because she was brought to us by a friend who, per usual, may or may not be sure what we do, but he knew it dealt with credit cards.

One night at my house on its well-known weekly Cigar Night, he told us a story about this fine lady in a pinch. Is that something we can handle? I had no idea. He'd have to describe the pinch. Does it require someone stunningly good-looking? If so, I could probably help.

No, no, it had to do with her taking credit cards. Great, a possible client. No, as it turns out, her business had closed and was not opening back up. She was on the outset of eighty, if not in her nineties, and was getting charged for her machine month after month (insert *Jaws* theme in my mind). Okay, so she closed the shop for good, had a credit card machine, and was still getting charged for it? Yes.

A lease. Unless his data was off, it was a lease. Boy, if I had just been born a little dumber, I could have set up leases!

This is a dirty pool. Drink that in and understand it is a dirty, dirty "they are perfectly okay with it" pool. These contracts are unconscionable. There is no way you can validate that unless your sole thought in life is that *you don't want to ever go backward, even one dime. I don't care who it burns. I will get them to sign.* Mephisto is laughing and thinking, was he ever so young to use his style of contracts? These do so much more damage.

I am going to use some ugly language here. No swearing, but specifically the word slave. Prepare.

There is an underlying thing in the industry, especially personal credit cards, that is used as a means of bringing in money for businesses. They want people to have more than they can handle. They want you over the tipping point. What is the tipping point? The tipping point is I can afford this. I can stop making purchases and slowly but surely pay this down even though they will be adding interest charges. I can get out. The far side of that mountain's tipping point, the point where you have crossed over, is not so nice.

On the other side, you can't afford it. You can barely handle your minimums. That's when they have you. They have a fish hook in you. It doesn't go through your mouth; it goes through your wallet. Now, you're the same thing as an indentured servant. I like to speak in hyperbole when having a drink with friends and expounding on something silly or odd, but in cases like this, one must keep their reserve. If you don't remember your history, an indentured servant is effectively a slave—a financial slave, but a slave nonetheless. When someone wanted passage to the New World to escape the old one, they often couldn't afford the exorbitant cost. Real estate on a ship is at a premium, and every slot and space had a cost. So, people who wanted to escape the drudgery of the Old World would have someone pay their way and work for them for seven years—seven years—for free except for room and board. You would be their financial slave. This was a wise choice for many people who bought passage with *future labor*, but the costs could not be ignored.

Let me say this another way. I want to buy something with money I don't yet have, so I will—by my work—be paying for this for years. Am I talking about New World passage, or am I speaking of credit card purchases? That is something you have to decide for yourself.

In this case, to sell her goods, a woman signed a contract saying that she would be on the hook for a four-year minimum in an unbreakable contract at some ungodly rate a month. I happen to know the rate. You've heard it before. This woman was on the King of the Hill board for a while with the $99 monthly lease. Four years of $99 a month will be $1,200 a year or a total of $4,800 for a $250 machine.

If I was just a little dumber...

So, I called my attorney—not my *main* attorney. That is my father. Yes, he scoffs and gets annoyed, but his ultimate interest is my best interest. No, this man works with him, and I go to him for various things. Personally, I think one needs a license to carry this man's number around. If it goes off, things happen, and I absolutely was calling on this.

"So, let me get this straight," he was already half up to steam. "This woman has a store or *had* one. It's closed now."

"Yes," I replied.

"And she is in her late eighties or so, pays $99 a month on a machine that is $250.00 brand new, on a fixed income, and they won't release her?"

"No. Most leases are unbreakable, but in this industry, most things that are locked in break if the business closes for good, like a term of a contract for the merchant account itself."

"What do you get out of it? If she magically gets out of this lease, she's not signing with you, right? I mean, her business is closed—for good."

"Yeah, closed for good. We get nothing."

"You just want her out of a really bad deal?"

"Yep," I told him. Maybe I felt like a cowboy.

"I'm all in. Don't worry, I'll get the dog to let go of this *particular* bone."

"Awesome. Let me know how it goes."

"And Will," he added. "There will be no charge."

Amazing. He would fight to get this done, and he wouldn't even use billable hours. He called me back two days later with two words: "It's done." I'd feel bad about it, but this guy is on the side of the angels. I never heard from the lady, nor did I need to. We heard about the need, went in, did what we could, and resolved it. Whatever her fixed income was, it now had an additional $99 a month staying home with her rather than flying away on eagles' wings.

5

A LITTLE OFF THE TOP?

Sometimes, it's depressing to think of all the ways people get taken in for something as paltry as money. Don't get me wrong. I love money in my pocket. It gives health, vigor, and youth to the step. That said, it is the lowest thing to wantonly defraud people. How much is a good night's sleep worth? I've had people ask me some ridiculous things. Ridiculous. One person asked me about leasing machines. I told them that we did not, nor would we ever, lease a machine. They are cheap and plentiful, and half the time, the processor will give them away. If not, they can be bought brand new for very little or refurbished for even less. In an all-out need, they can even be rented.

"What if I said that I would walk away if I can't get a lease?" Yes, that was once asked. I'll use no names to protect the guilty.

"Then, we would walk away," I answered.

"Why?"

"Because I will never sign a bad deal for the customer. It doesn't matter if they want it. Besides the ethics of it all, it would be bad business. As a specialist, I am to tell you what you need, not what you want to hear. If accountants caved to clients' whims, many would be in jail. The real shame is that a lease would bring my firm a wad of cash, and we still won't sign them, and you think that's a bad thing."

So now we come to the Barber Supply Store. Oh, I liked this old cuss. He was fun and rambunctious and would volunteer information at the drop of a dime and give you the whole back story. In places that smell like old barber shops, a good story, and the scented nostalgia quickly take you back in time and space. But they were going to be closing down in a couple of months. They were getting on in years, and the children didn't want the business. Still, a woman who worked there asked me to look over some statements, "You know... just in case."

Looking at their statements was like watching an episode of *Mutual of Omaha's Wild Kingdom* after the predator had grabbed an herbivore. It was not in a good state of affairs. I know what fees are, but it became problematic. We asked if they owned the machine or if they saw any payments coming from their checking account. They had an answer for that: They had a fee come out for $129 a month or so (or so?), and they didn't know what it was for, but they think it was for support—maybe.

May I see it? Yes, I could. After some fumbling, they found it and showed me. By this point, you have to know that if a group was charging a very small business $129 in fees for support, I am going to bust that up like a video game's ending explosion. It was worse than that. It had nothing—and I mean nothing—to do with their processor, bank, or merchant account. I will never know how they got involved in it, but it was all a scam.

They believe they had gotten a postcard telling them that their merchant account had an issue and they could have it fixed. So, you know, postcard phishing. This is when I need a drink and someone to commiserate with. Well, not yet; I still have to do this.

Here is something that I learned from a bank while sitting in a bank with a bank officer I knew. She was one of the people I would take to lunch, and as I was called CLO for my company (Chief Lunch Officer), it was a role I took seriously. What I would tell someone was simply, "Look, I am going to buy somebody lunch today. It might as well be you." A happy stomach makes a happy person. You spend 85 percent of the time talking about family and what you will do this weekend, and more importantly, their family and what they will do this weekend. Pretty soon, you're an okay person because even if they positively cannot use your services, you're not wasting their time. A person has to eat, right? Then, later, if they can work with you, they will let you know (if you buy lunch).

A bank can yank back *any* funds that were moved electronically for up to sixty days. A great example is a gym that I stopped going to. Well, you must let them know so they can stop the automatic draft. How much time? Thirty days. Thirty days? That's okay; I'll use the gym for another month. No. I couldn't use the gym, as I was canceling. Then, I'd be paying for a month that I can't use the gym. That was the plan, Stan. Yeah, but that's not going to work for me. Bill me the last month. I am stopping service now. I go to the bank and inform the young woman that what I am about to ask her to do I know she can do legally, so please don't tell me she can't. "Yank back my last payment. They want a free month of fees but are not getting it from me." Done. Don't play at fisticuffs if the other guy is Mohamed Ali.

So, I told the owner of the Barber Supply that I knew his bank. I knew them well. I was going there, and I would tell them what to do with his account. I then told him that they were, of course, going to say that only he could do it. That's when I would be telling a man I have taken to lunch more than once to pick up the phone and call Barber Supply and get his authorization. The important things were to 1) be waiting on that call and 2) tell them you authorize them to do basically whatever the heck it is that Will says as long as it puts money back in the account, not take any out (for safety reasons).

And that's what I did. That's what the bank manager did, and that is what the owner of Barber Supply did. The bank manager was able to reach back far enough to get well over $400 and put it back in Barber Supply's account, and I saved him over $100 on his normal account. His savings were about $230 a month. They were so happy with that and having the money back in the account that they switched to me and stayed open for three and a half more years. Even if he hadn't switched, I still would have done all the leg work to save him those monies and put them back in his account, but getting him so he could stay open a few more years was a feather in my cap that I love to swish around.

6

SAMURAI DO WHAT NOW?

I hesitate to mention this. Still, it's all about the process; sometimes, that is all about the ask. You'll never know how much business is out there for nothing more than a simple ask.

I have done some writing outside of my comfort zone, and I have been published in *The Art of Manliness,* an online magazine with eight million readers that has also published a couple of books. Brett McKay and his wife, Kate, started the whole concept, as he was a bit rugged, an individualist, loved being self-reliant, and, yes, manly. And she likes manly men. The articles and pieces are fun, motivating, and often written together by him and his wife. She is not a trodden-down woman, and neither is he a spineless jellyfish. It's a great site and not the phallocentric He-Man Woman Hater's Club from *the Little Rascals.* It's just a site for men about how to be strong, self-reliant, and self-challenging. I was introduced to it by friends, developed a great curiosity about it, and started reading a lot on the site. I even had an idea, but unfortunately, it was stated that they were no longer taking outside submissions.

Dang it. But then, I realized I was a grown man, and many things are there for the asking. So, I wrote my article. I will tell you what it is, but please do not throw the book down as being ludicrous. It was a title that was both truthful and made to get people's attention so they would read it. I can't make this up. Actually, I can, and I did come up with it. I mean, I am not lying or pretending. This can be read via Google right now. "How to Poop Like a Samurai" was an idea I got from reading a book years earlier entitled *The Autumn Lightning*. It is a true story about a ten-year-old boy who found a Samurai sword master in his hometown.

Later, he would learn to exercise his bowels like a Samurai. That part is less important, but it is real. However, the thing I focus on here is the asking. His asking had to be coupled with persistence, and I'll tell you why. There are certain masters, and in Japan, this was a very real thing; they did not want just any paying student. Imagine turning away people who will pay you to teach them. It's like being in the Ivy League for teachers. No, they would turn you away. When your time is valuable, you take real and very persistent students.

The young man in question heard there was a swordsman in his neighborhood. He heard it like I heard the aliens fly down in UFOs whenever we were not looking. So, he went on his search and found that, yes, a Japanese family lived a few streets over. He went over there the following day, knocked on the door, and was greeted by a Japanese woman. It was awkward because how do you ask for a swordsman? He tells her he is looking for a sword master (as almost every ten-year-old boy is). She is polite and tells him there is no one there to help him. She didn't say "No," nor did she say he had the wrong house. He excused himself.

He came back the next day. There was no one there to help him. He didn't know what it was, but she was not brusque or curt. It sounded like she didn't really want to send him away either, but she just stood there. Every day, day after day, even in the rain, he kept coming back. She was sorry, but there was no one there to help him. This was years ago, but I remember that this went on for a few months, upward of six. He kept showing up. He kept knocking. He kept asking.

One day, months into an ordeal that most of us would have abandoned, she opened the door and stood aside, saying that he should go into the next room. From that moment on, he would be a lifelong student of the swordsman that he had heard a rumor about. He would tell you he was being trained even from that first day, and he would not be wrong. He would learn the art of the sword, how to speak Japanese, and even how to go number two like a Samurai, but the real training was always in the ask and the persistence. I tell you this because most issues in business—be it with your clients or a business you use—are fixable or attainable for no more than asking and persisting.

I did this with Brett and his wife, the owners of *The Art of Manliness*. Who cares what the sign says? Not taking any more outside submissions became a personal challenge. So, what did I do?

The first thing I did was write the dang article. I was not going in there empty-handed. More business has been won because they had already done the work and were submitting it. For the person or company you are selling to, it's a bird in the hand, my friend. A bird in the hand. You're not selling theoretical; you're selling an actual thing. So, I wrote it. I wrote it, and I re-wrote it. I made it what I wanted it to be. I double-checked all grammar. I read and re-read it, so every turn of phrase did its job. I didn't want a clumsy thing that would have to be patched and fixed.

Finally, it was done. Now what? Well, I had to get it to them. Again, I wanted this to be as simple as possible. They had a physical address, so I wrote a letter. Yes, an actual hand-written, wet-signed letter. I alluded to things about him, his wife, his children, and certain articles to let him know I read his site. Things that he said or certain popular pieces go a long way in that regard. I also included in that letter my desire to submit an article, a printed copy of the article so he could read it right there, and a flash drive with a soft copy of the article so he had to do no real work to upload it and use it if he so chose. The thing I was shooting for was to make it easy—make it easy, make it really easy.

You may think that a printed copy of the article was unnecessary. You'd be wrong. It let him see the article, its size and scope, and, of course, read the title right at the top in bold font and centered on the page:

"How to Poop Like a Samurai"

If nothing else, one's morbid sense of curiosity was being highly leveraged here. I wanted him to see it. I wanted him to read it. If he just read that part, I had a feeling he would read the rest.

He did.

He wrote back to me and *loved* the article. He thought it was witty, funny, and informative. He and his wife thought that while it was a real thing, it had just enough tongue-in-cheek to engage and get people reading. We worked back and forth over the next week and a half as he engaged an artist (with my permission... What was I going to say? No? Please, I wanted all this) and had me proof pictures of a fully armored Samurai sitting on a modern toilet. It was fun and highly read. His exact words to me were that the article was "wildly popular." Numbers-wise, I think it was his most popular article of 2014. The comments on it alone scrolled down for what would be pages and pages.

Many people got lost on the idea that a Samurai would not be on a modern potty. Yeah, no kidding. Sorry, you missed the joke. That was just for fun and to show how one might go to the bathroom in modern times in the fashion that Samurai were taught. They did not have modern toilets, much less the modern plumbing that would make said toilet function. Forest through the trees, people. Don't miss the forest through the trees.

7

JUST ASK

I say this for real, tangible reasons. The irreverently titled article was not the point. The fact that there was a non-sentient gatekeeper in the statement "No longer taking outside submissions" made untold people shy away. To me, it was a challenge. I won that challenge. I won it for almost no more than the ask. Yes, a little persistence, too, but basically, the ask. A case not dissimilar was the $1 Million a Month Car Dealership. It was the third business we spoke to in the vein of what we do, and it was a huge win, but it almost wasn't.

The agent who was approaching was getting blown off. Remember, they had (and have) a small army of bookkeepers. He didn't know what to do. It's an ask situation, and it requires a little persistence. The boy who would study from the Samurai swords master asked and kept asking. He got in. Why not keep trying? Don't be rude, but ask. Ask again.

I have a great dog—really. *Really*, really. She's a Boston Terrier, and Boston Terriers are not cheap. I got her *for the ask*. I was at my grandfather's house, and his girlfriend's daughter (true story, don't ask) was there with her Boston Terrier. She was simply the best dog in the world—sweet, playful, demur, yet excited. Even non-dog people compliment this dog. The second time I saw her, I said I would readily take her if they ever wanted to get rid of this dog. They huffed, and I said, "Really." A year later, they called and asked if I was serious. I wanted to know if *they* were serious. No one—*no one*—gives up this dog. She is practically a show animal.

As it turns out, she was the dog of a couple, the husband of which had died. She was more his dog. Now, the wife didn't know what to do. The only thing I said was, "When do you want me to pick her up?" Personally, I thought it was like saying, "If you ever want to give away your Ferrari…"

She did, and I got her. Hallelujah. There's a point to this.

8

SEA CHANGE

A sea change is a major shift or profound change in something or what is being done. A mentor of mine calls it a pivot. Sometimes, you pivot in business. The quarterback, looking for someone open to throw to, looks and sees a guy not in his immediate line of fire, pivots so he can throw to the guy who's open, and throws. A sea change is not unlike this. It's an allusion to *The Tempest* by Shakespeare.

> *Full fathom five thy father lies,*
> *Of his bones are coral made;*
> *Those are pearls that were his eyes.*
> *Nothing of him that doth fade,*
> *But doth suffer a sea-change*
> *Into something rich and strange.*
> *Sea-nymphs hourly ring his knell:*
> *Ding-dong.*
> *Hark! Now I hear them—ding-dong, bell.*

It refers to a man who drowns in about thirty feet of water as a fathom is six feet. I say this because sometimes one's approach must change due to differences in business and personality. Simply put, just because they said no or passed doesn't mean they can't use it; it might mean you didn't tell them the right way.

Years ago, a wine company sponsored a mystery television show. They invested a lot of money, but sales were going nowhere fast. The problem was it was a good show. Mysteries are like that. They get you all tied up and thinking about them, whether it's a fictional piece or you are watching NBC's *Dateline* on Friday. Money wasn't an issue. What could it be? Also, they did not have a butler.

Do you see what happens? You get so twisted about the issue that you are not thinking about the commercial. You get a drink and some chocolate because it's when you and the spouse sit down; all the kids are finally zonked out. Maybe you quickly run to the bathroom so you can get back and get comfortable. You are not thinking about wine. It becomes a situation where your company sponsors a show that is too good to help you. People are there and watching. They are doing it intently. They just can't pay attention to you.

The wine company pulled the plug on that one and sponsored a show more in the line of a round table discussion. It was boring in comparison, but wine sales went upwards of 1,000 percent in some demographics. Who knew?

I have been speaking with a businessperson who could not talk to me right now about this and saving money (wait for it) because he needed to concentrate on "how to save his business some money right now." I can't make that up. Go back and read that again. I'll wait here. Done? How does one even answer that? If you say, "This is about saving you money," it can be too aggressive and make the person feel like you're arguing. How can you talk about saving money when the person can't because they have to save money? This man was drowning, and he knew it.

People do not pay attention. Ask me how I know. For one, I don't pay attention. I have a business, a foundation, a wife, and two kids whose favorite thing to eat is cash salad. Chomp, chomp, chomp. I'm busy, and when you are talking to me, I will glaze over and think about dinner, what I have to do in foundational paperwork, or the next piece in that 1964 BSA motorcycle I'm going to polish and restore. That's the human condition. Don't judge. You have the same disease to one degree or another.

The best and most notable example I can ever use is something that happened a thousand times. In my past life working with credit card processing software and speaking to banks and providers daily about what they can do, how they can be offered, and what needs to be implemented, I would get emails that would read like this:

> *Will,*
> *Hey, just a quick email. Does Softcharge take multiple users?*
>
> *Thanks,*
> *~Busy Person in the Financial Sector*

My response would be very short to mirror their time restraints but still helpful.

> *Hey Busy Person,*
> *Yes. Softcharge can do multiple users.*
> *Let me know if you need anything else.*
>
> *Best regards,*
> *~Will*

Now, this is an important question. Did you get lost in my response? Was it convoluted in any way? Did you take a mental misstep at any time in all the rabbit trails of conversations we had going on there? Some of you will think I am making this up. I almost wish I was. Many of you will say, "Oh my gosh! Will and I have the same client!" Read on, friend, and see their follow-up.

Will,

Thanks for getting back to me so quickly.

Hey, did you ever get a chance to find out about that multi-user question?

Let me know,

~Busy and Not Paying Any Attention at All

Did I get a chance to find out about that multi-user question? Are you high? What in Heaven's name were you thanking me for if not for answering the question? You had one question. I gave you one response and a "reach out if you need anything else," but you are already confused. Seriously. A basic rule in conversation is that at least *one person* must pay attention. Also, it should be, at a minimum, the person asking. Let me know if I am off base, but I don't think this is something we need to ask "Dear Abby" about.

Here's the second issue. It happened all the time—like several times a week. I was at a point where I was ready to stop popping Excedrin and instead just start injecting it behind my eyeball. I would start leaving people quick voice mails if I couldn't get them on the phone and shoot them the response email as a backup. It sometimes helped, but that's the world for you. We are a busy people. We are the proverbial ant bed that the kid just gave a swift kick to. We often feel like we are the only ones trying to put Humpty Dumpty back together again. Can you hear me, Lord? It's me, Will.

The guy who was too busy because he was trying to save his business money wasn't flat-out insane. He was just in more of a fight-or-flight mode than I was. It's easy in mid-panic to not see the forest through the trees, and this guy couldn't see the Grand Canyon because of that big hole in the ground.

We needed a sea change. So, instead of telling him along the lines of, "Golly, sir, that's what I'm trying to do," I hit him from a side wind.

"I understand," I said as if wrapping up. "We can talk in a few months, and I'll show you how the system bleeds you of a few hundred extra dollars a month. Thanks for your time."

"Wait! What?" he asked quickly to catch me before I was off the phone.

"What, 'What?'" I asked.

"What did you say about the system taking a few hundred dollars a month?"

"Oh, yes. Right. Well, the system is designed to move up incrementally. Most people have a few hundred, and sometimes a thousand, a month go out. It's a big expenditure to cut as soon as possible. I'll follow up when you have a little more time, sir."

"Well, I mean, I have a few minutes now. I guess I can talk."

"I don't want to pester you, sir. You might not be ready to chat just yet. What I show business owners is how I get my multi-million-dollar clientele. It's how they stay very streamlined and agile. It's a growth factor." Okay, maybe I did draw that out. It wasn't as bad as the owner telling Doofus he had to pay in cash. Maybe it was a little vanity, but I wanted him awake.

"Well…"

"If you're sure you have a couple of minutes, we can do some basic work, but to really cut out your overspending, I'd need you to email in a current statement. That way, I can have a bunch of math geeks—and I mean people with *no* discernable personalities whatsoever—crawl over and deep dive into your statement. They'll shave it so close it'll be red from the razor burn."

"Oh, yeah? Really?" Now, he was paying attention.

"Yeah. You know, that would be quicker for you right now. That way, you could get back to what you're doing, and I could have my guys working on this while you're working on that."

That statement came in, and he saved $2,500 that year. Did it save his business? No, he wasn't in dire straits, but it did help energize him a lot. He could now do his work with a clear mind and, dare I say, a little sunshine. Yes, I dare it.

9

YOU DON'T REALLY NEED
TO REALLY READ IT

At what point is someone jaded? In their field, it's probably faster than in other less-walked-in areas. If "Use makes mastery," then when we judge being jaded, "Use rushes mastery In."

I was inside an antique dealer here in my hometown years ago. They have schranks in there for $20 grand. If you're not used to that term, you have no military in your family from the seventies or eighties. *Schrank* means closet, but there is always something lost in translation. Really, it's a wall unit used like a great cabinet that will house and hold almost everything you own in and on a single wall. It is ordered, precise, and made in a multitude of styles, many of which resemble coo-coo clocks in their woodwork. I mean that in a good way.

The owner and his nephew are skilled in their eye for pieces and what they and their clients want. They can explain every piece and most of the pieces' provenance in detail. They know their stuff, and you will pay for their knowledge. The issue is that skill does not leap from one field to another.

I was quoting them one day when the nephew had to tell me that the other guy's numbers were lower. That is going to happen. Luckily, I am not that style of commodity anymore, which is nothing but a race to zero. Still, I knew many groups lead with a great rate and yank it away later. That is harder to explain to people and can seem aggressive. More on that later. For now, I simply asked if I might see the numbers, as I had put a good foot forward.

He pulled out the quote and handed it to me. This is what I saw that fine day:

Chk Crd	1.50
Crd Crd	1.99
Rds Crd	2.99

I quoted him 1.60 percent, and he returned with this blistering piece of trash. This is where you want to laugh, scream, point fingers, or even say you have a paint-by-numbers canvas. Would they like to buy that at $10,000? You'd like to, but you don't. Let's put this side by side.

Theirs	vs.	Ours
Chk Crd	1.50	0.87
Crd Crd	1.99	1.60
Rds Crd	2.99	2.40

Does that help?

You see, he looked at the very top, did no math—no real study or even partial study—and saw that 1.50 is less than 1.60.

I explained that "Chk Crd" was, of course, a debit card or check card. The other guys put it at the top, but it wasn't their main fee. Their store did all credit cards and rewards cards. What the other guys wanted for debit cards was almost double the rate, and what they wanted for a credit card was forty basis points (really thirty-nine, but who's counting?) overcharged.

10

THREE CARD MONTY
STRIKES AGAIN

In my teens, I was replacing a nut from a pair of skates. I held it up to my grandfather, who said it was a 5/8^{ths} self-locking nut. He barely looked at it. That was because he was a farmer. He had been born into a life of self-sufficiency. He didn't need to look deeply at the nut because he knew it. He knew it like you know your (*insert here something you use daily*). Yeah, just like that. Use makes mastery, as the old saying goes.

I glanced at the sheet with his rates on it and could see those letters easily, as you can now. He looked at them the way I look at most insurance quotes. He stares at it, gets a headache, fears he is somehow inducing an aneurism in his brain, and then puts it down. He just took the easy path, saw the number floating on top, and went with it. There is a psychological term for that, and it's called "not-wanting-to-deal-with-all-this-garbage."

This happens more than one can guess. I have told people back in the day to send in their entire statement. If there is a blank page, especially send it in because I have seen items typed in half-grayscale at the top or bottom to look like a header or footer, respectively, that would cost them an extra $500 a year. The half-grayscale trick makes your eyes float over and ignore it, like that pile of laundry on the floor. If you step past it twice, it is now invisible. Companies know that your brain—just like that poor baby elephant's—has been trained to ignore headers and footers. Trained and trained well. Why would you look? They're often there and do nothing, right?

When was the last time you read a traffic sign? I mean, really read it? Well, they are designed not to have to be read. They can be used even if you are illiterate or dropped your glasses, like Velma from Scooby Doo. A red octagon with a white border and white letters: stop sign. Yellow triangle: caution and the picture describes what's up. The government always uses the same patterns as they have taught everyone how to use them. Now, your brain takes no deciphering and does it automatically. It's why in some communities where they change the signage to use their colors to better blend in, those signs do not legally bind the driver. They are not the legal pattern and colors.

One must train the mind to read even the junk at the top and the bottom, the silly junk emails that sign away your rights, and the pages on contracts that look unimportant. "The clouded mind sees nothing," said the old radio drama *The Shadow*. Of course, Lamont Cranston also said, "Who knows what evil lurks in the heart of men?" Sometimes, I wonder.

11

NICE CARPET

I have known more than one bank manager, but I bought a lot of lunches. I have known good ones, busy ones who barely look up, and ones with part of their last meal still in their mouths. True story.

I also know more than one who got "called on the carpet" because of merchant accounts. Where exactly that phrase came from is in the fog. Supposedly, carpet was originally the covering of the table, like in the conference room, so it meant something was under consideration. However, the first use of this particular idiom was purportedly from 1902, when people in the main office—or better yet, head office—were rich enough to have carpet as a floor covering. Thus, to be called on was to stand before a boss to answer for something directly.

It wasn't good then, and it's not good now.

These particular bank managers got called on the carpet for doing the unthinkable: saying they wouldn't do something that made the bank money. One woman I worked with would tell such a tale about this; she would get angrier with every re-telling. As her story went, she said she wasn't signing any more merchant accounts. This made the powers that be grind to a dead stop to get her to give them a really good reason why. She had one: It was destroying her reputation.

How? She told them quite simply that in the zeal to get accounts and to keep the machine running at peak efficiency, she was forbidden to speak to her clients about their merchant accounts. Why would she? It was done. They were in the system being ground down into cash. The best use of her time was... setting up more merchant accounts. *No!* She was ultimately building a portfolio, as any business should be doing. Building a level of knowledge and trust with every client and then being told not to contact them and not to be contacted by them. (I think I saw this movie called *Erin Brockovich,* but that's another story.)

She said she had lost the trust of innumerable clients she could easily have handled and did not even have to fix the problem; she had just to be their liaison. She was denied that, so instead of building a portfolio, she was building a broken road of no longer trusting clients. Simply put, she was becoming a bad guy in people's eyes for not being allowed to help. She would end up leaving that bank and going to another where she was spot on in her work and had me as her bank's specialist.

12

TIED AND TETHERED

If you're in the banking industry, I'm not speaking ill of you or even of banks. You know yourself as we all do of our companies and industries, each with its own assets and deficits. Sadly, to be more efficient, sometimes a group will do the very harm they mean to correct. I've done a lot of business with banks over the years. There is good, and there is bad. Let you and I be the good.

Sometimes, though, we use our jobs like sticks and carrots to lead a stubborn mule of a client to where we need him to be. I prefer the carrot. Most businesses do, but many take a stick and paint it to look like a carrot. For example, one time, I was consulting for a music store.

Actually, it was a chain of five music stores, and we got them to send in their statements. It should have been in garbage bags with all the blood coming out. I'd like to say that we poured over this for days and days like mysterious mountain trolls forging mystical weapons of rare elements. I'd like to say that, but it was an afternoon, and I wasn't even involved. My partner did it completely. So, when he came back in and told me that they were overpaying $18,000 a year, I was overjoyed.

"That's fantastic!" I told him—not that I wanted a possible client to suffer, but a mechanic needs broken cars. "On top of that, I was told that their bank had just *lowered* them 'because they were such a good client.'" We both laughed at that old chestnut. They were lowered—to only overpaying $18,000 a year.

The CFO nearly cried when I told him. Cried bad, not good. I was in an alien land. It's one thing to not believe you're overpaying that much and to make me show you. It's one thing to have a healthy paranoia and think I'll save them that money for a little while, then jerk it back up. But that was not his issue.

"He'll never switch," he said.

"Who?" I asked.

"Ted, the owner." No, Ted is not his real name. The names have been changed to protect the foolish.

"Why not? If $18 grand is no big deal, please give me a spare $18 grand. Heck. Give me $9,000 and keep the difference—a big win for both of us." Yes, I did say that.

"You don't understand," I wanted to tell him my dad would like to have him in his my-son-is-still-a-kid support group. "Ted won't leave because they have our line of credit, and there is one of these banks in all of our five locations. We're tied up."

This is where a reasonable person wants to ask why they were invited in. That's a question that people who make less ask. As my old manager used to say, "You can feed your pride, or you can feed your family. Pick *one*." Instead, I sat back and poured long, slow poison in his ear. Hamlet's uncle Claudius would have been so jealous.

I told him how my daddy always told me to "Vote with my feet." If I wasn't being treated right, I could go where I would be. I could vote with my feet. That has always stuck with me.

At the end of the day, being overcharged $18,000 annually on a merchant account to keep a line of credit is being overcharged $18,000 on a line of credit. That's $1,500 a month more than whatever percentage your company pays now. (Don't think I am that good at math. I just had an over-charged per month in the report.) There are nine banks down the road that would salivate like Pavlovian dogs at the chance to get your line of credit and the interest that goes with it. In the meantime, you get to pay them $18,000 a year to have the honor of a line of credit with them—you, an established business with five stores. I could probably get a commission to get three banks in here to bid on your line of credit. As for the bank near each one, I wouldn't pay $18,000 for the use of it. That's a car. I use two banks.

13

YOU'RE NOT THE ONLY ONE

I am glad I took the time with that client. I could have been like the other businesses that the car dealer chased off and not gotten the business. Now, I see this every day. A bank that ties you down like that is not the bank to be trusted.

Is that dangerous to say? I said it. Anytime you're locked down, all the other group has to say is their old refrain, "Well, your contract doesn't end until..." which is the same as saying, "You're not important to us until..."

It's one thing to have a line of credit and the bank loan on your building or business tethered if the rates are market comparable. Even that is too expensive if you will pay it out three times over in fees. Nothing is worth that.

14

WE'VE GOT YOUR MACHINE

I've said this before, and it bears some mild repeating here. It doesn't matter who bought your machine. They can take their machine and go home if they don't like it. Machines are a dime a dozen. They are cheap, easy, and plentiful. The idea of being held up by your machine is like standing on the beach and someone telling you that if you don't do as they say, they will walk away with their *handful of sand*. That one handful. In the meantime, you are standing there, toes in the sand. Sand to your left, right, forward, and behind. If you reach down and scoop it up, there's even sand under the dang water. You might need to dry it out, but it's still sand.

The number of times clients have called and said that their bank owns their machine and they are now stuck is like grains of sand on the beach. That's when you tell them that, for all intents and purposes, their new account comes with a new machine so that silly old one that may or may not be nearing the end of its life can be deeply well-wished as it heads off to the graveyard of bank terminals.

15

CAUSE YOU'LL GIVE IT TO ME

I was sitting in the office of the senior investment banker for a national bank. His office was off the offices of his bank's branch here in my hometown. If you listen, you just might hear the Spanish Moss rustling as it hangs like an old man's beard from the live Oak trees. I'm sitting there thinking that I could effectively throw frisbees in this guy's office or at least hold a major paper airplane competition. It was huge—twelve-foot ceilings with rich colors of rugs and wallpapers. All the things that if you are going to have a bank invest for you, your office better have. This was one Dapper Dan with a full-on, hand-tied cloth bowtie so you could feel Old South money flowing through his office.

The odd thing was that he had called me. Could I come to see him? Why, yes, I could, and here I was. We chatted for a moment. Then, pleasantries aside, he told me how he owned some high-end rental property and needed a merchant account and a machine. My Spidey sense was going off mildly but still going off. It should be ringing in my ears like the worst case of tinnitus you've ever heard of, but it wasn't. It was just saying, "Be aware."

Eventually, I had to crack into the conversation with a bit of a sobering statement.

"So, I have to ask," I started.

"Ask what?" he asked in return.

"Well, you are at a bank. You're with a bank. I mean, you physically are at a bank and with them. You're, in fact, the bank."

"I'm not *the* bank. I am with the bank," he answered. He wasn't sure where I was going.

"Sir, I am happy to set you up. The question is, why me? Why at all? You're here at this bank. You wouldn't even need to walk down to them. I bet if you called, one of them would happily trot down here and set you up."

"I suppose."

"Granted, they'd do it on the same processor I would. But why?"

"Ah! Yes. Well, that's easy, Will." I wish it was so I already knew the answer. I took the appointment, as I don't say no to business unless it breaks a moral threshold. Yet, I hadn't figured it out. It must be easy with a particular piece of knowledge he was about to let loose.

"You do everything that everyone else doesn't. You'll give me what my bank would charge me $750.00 for."

You will never know the level of professionalism it took and that I displayed to maintain a sense of decorum at that moment. I nearly coughed up a dad-blamed lung, but alas, I did not.

His bank, which he was a major player for, charged $750 for a machine they probably got in bulk at less than $200 a piece and sold for a profit in the three to three-and-a-half-fold range.

The real story carries substantially more venom than at first perceived. The first thing was that the bank wouldn't at least sell him one at cost as a banking insider. How crazy is that? The amount of money this guy brought to the bank, and they can't get him one at cost. It's bad business. How many times does this guy think, while sitting in front of major clients and businesses, that his bank would overcharge them and risk his relationship? The second is that if he can't get it at a reasonable price, the Joe-off-the-street can't either.

Finally, and worst of all, this sets a poison in people's minds that is hard to uproot. This is the baby elephant's memory and the preprogramming of our eyes on the road signs: Those machines are rare commodities to be prized, possessed, and not given up lightly, especially after one has paid the better part of $1,000 for one.

16

CAR DEALER GONE BAD

That brings us to the third car dealership I ever sat in front of. We did not sign them.

We were still heady with all the wind in our sales from closing two car dealerships in two months. They had been the first two we had spoken to, and we closed both. We knew what to do. We knew what to say. We had one sexy offer, and if you're thinking along the proverbial lines of "Pride goeth before the fall," brother, you don't know the half of it.

We were introduced as we had been to the others. We were getting to the point that this was a layup given to us so we could come in and dunk it. The old alley-oop was in play, and we were heading down the court. Our high tops were laced, and we were ready.

Could we do this? We did this every day. Can we do that? That is our bread and butter and helps differentiate us from our competitors. There were minor snags, mind you, as they always were. We had been working with the eldest son up to a certain point. Then, we had to eventually get to the numbers. After all, it doesn't matter what kind of layup someone gives you. If you cost too much, you're no longer in the game.

We had to go through the old man's assistant to get the numbers. That was like making the whole sale over again.

Why did we need the numbers? Why were we doing this? Who told me to follow up with her? She was apparently with the company and right under the dragon's wing a little too long, as she had lost a sense of professionalism that I had with a dealership that dwarfed them.

The much larger group had an older woman there who they jokingly said they inherited, and she would always have a position there as long as she wanted. That woman regularly called me by name, and once, on an appointment that I got to twenty-four hours early (all my fault), she apologized because she was afraid she had made a mistake. So did the big, *big* GM's executive assistant and the big, *big* GM. Again, it was all my fault. At least I was a day early rather than a day late.

Classy people.

This woman was not that. She was annoyed and let me know but eventually relented. I can deal with that. If you don't want the crazy, you can't have clients. I got the numbers. We showed that we could save them thousands. We did all the paperwork. The last thing would be to deal with the dad—senior, not junior.

My father once told me about a man who saw thieves in every shadow and around every corner. This guy spent more of the county's money he worked for looking for thieves than he ever did trying to get any work done. He never found anything either—not that you could convince him, though. Dad said he had been like that all his life and had been on any of the people he knew radar. He was just this crazy guy who was *sure* that everyone was trying to take terrible advantage of the system and people all the time. He said he would never be convinced either, at least not on this side of the grave.

Why were we even having that conversation? Well, we had a piece of property that had a bunch of abandoned beautiful oak pews in—pews, as in church pews. The long wooden benches you sit on while pondering your life or watching that couple get married. Rather than have them hauled off, I asked for my father's (earthly father) blessing to handle the pews myself. He let me, and I called a few pastors and asked if they knew of any burgeoning churches that might want a nice set of oak pews but don't have the money.

They came up with some names, and I called them all. I mean all. I told them about the pews, and most were curious, but some were looking a gift horse in the mouth. I was getting sorry I had asked this particular boon. Still, my spiel was the same. Time was a factor. This was a first come, first served situation. There was absolutely no charge. The property had to be empty by a certain date, so these would have to be gone.

Several groups came by and looked, window shopped. Again, high gift horse mouth-being-looked-at goings on. There was easily $10,000 in pews, and groups were kicking tires. I reminded each one that time was of the essence. This was a first come, first served situation, as in whoever says, "I'll take them," gets them. They all left after a few minutes.

Several days later, a group said they loved them and would send a truck. Awesome. I was glad someone could put these beauties to use. We put them outside for legal reasons as a notice had been put in a paper, and the legal time limit had passed. The adoptive church of these pews then came by and picked up the abandoned-on-the-curb pews, and all was well in the world.

For two days…

That's when I got a call. It was from the second group that came by. I informed him that the pews were gone, as someone had decided to move on them. What? How could they be gone? Again, a group that looked at them decided they would very much like to have them and came and took them. The conversation was getting weird. Then, he stopped. He started asking less like, "Can I know why?" and more like a detective trying to find the dirt—all in an incredulous tone dripping with accusation and annoyance. Could I just tell him why he didn't get the pews? That's when you breathe, ignore all that someone implies, and review.

"Why, of course. As you remember from our initial phone conversation and when you came by almost a week after to look at them and are now calling a week after that, I said time was an issue. First come, first served. These people wanted the pews and moved quickly."

He could have easily had the pews if he had said he wanted them at the time of viewing and come back the following day with a truck. That had been two weeks prior. A little more was said, but it was all in the same vein. It was accepting it as it was now fact, but obviously, something odd was going on there. Maybe we had secretly never liked him, and other paranoias were tumbling about his head.

So, when I relayed this to Pappy, he asked me who it was, and I told him. That was when I was instructed that some people see a thief around every corner. Whether or not they were really there, the thief is always one step ahead.

I was about to meet a version of this guy all over again. It was Senior, not the son, at the car dealer. All I had to do was go in and get the papers signed. All the hard stuff had been done. I had worked with the son and answered all his questions. He loved the idea. I had worked with too-long-under-the-dragon's-wing and gotten all the data and information to prep the paperwork. All I needed was a signature.

The first issue was he wasn't prepped for my coming in. That alone was amazing. I had to work with staff over several weeks to get to this point. His assistant booked the time with me. How did he not know what it was about?

So, I go into the basics. We had been working with his son, gotten the assistant's data, and found thousands to save off their current numbers. That's when I got a flurry of questions. I have found it's normally an excitable person who glares about and asks numerous questions back-to-back like a drowning person gasping for oxygen. That's okay, as their money is just as green as the next guy's, and I was going to save him a comma worth of fees.

Well, he didn't understand. What's going on? What do I mean he's overpaying? If I wrote those all together with no punctuation, it would be more like the conversation I had. Slowly, as if letting the steam kettle come down from its whistling, I related all the key pieces. That's when I got the lie of all time—a lie he had been fed.

"Well, what about the guy I use now?" he asked.

"What about him?"

"What do I do about him?"

"He's overcharging your business thousands a year."

"Well, what am I supposed to do about him? I mean, he put half his own money in to cover the cost of these machines."

I could have seen this was a bit like the bull of a man, captain of industry situation all over again, but I handled it with more finesse.

"Sir, there used to be a certain cost to these machines, but in all fairness, a business of your size warrants that they should place the machines for free. As you can see from our paperwork, all your machines are free. I think they have been paid back in full for the amount they have overcharged your fully vested company. Any machine you get from me is absolutely free and should be so from anyone else."

Sadly, there was a lot of chagrin and red-faced glaring eyes in the room. I was later told that this individual had a long history of thinking everyone was trying to steal from him. The worst thing was he was partially right. The other guy didn't put half the money in for his machines. He lied. He said that to get the guy over a hump because he probably balked at the ludicrous price he was quoted, and the guy said he argued it down and would pay half.

No, he didn't.

How many lies are lying around out there, and people are simply accepting them as true? Not to hit you with a sermon, but if you lay out the truth and do a good job at your work, you will have customers aplenty. Nobody laid out any money for these machines other than the glaring-eyed owner—not a dime, nickel, or penny. In fact, I'd be a monkey's uncle if he didn't make money on the owner buying all these machines.

17

ELECTRON IS A GIRL'S NAME

I t really is. You hear it often, but *electron* is the Greek for the name we now know as Amber.

You're thinking that's a color, and it is. But it's named after a substance that is dried tree sap, which can harden over time. Once hardened, it can be broken off and polished into what some people mistake for a stone. It is often used in jewelry for its honeyed-yellow earth tones. You might even remember it from the movie *Jurassic Park* when the wealthy owner had a cane with an amber head and an embedded prehistoric mosquito. So, what in the heck does that have to do with girls and electricity?

There is a beginning to everything. A child's science experiment was, at one time, the greatest of things to ponder and study. So, what is it that children do? They (and by they, I mean me and absolutely you) took a balloon and rubbed it on their head at one time or another. Once this silly exercise in childish behavior of rubbing, frizzy hair, and squeaking balloon rubber was over, the child sets the balloon on a wall, watches it roll, adjust slightly, and then hang there exactly the way an automobile wouldn't.

Ladies and gentlemen, may I introduce static electricity?

We all know this and have done it. Oh, to return to simpler times. However, at one time, this was a novel idea. There were no balloons, but it was still done. The ancient Greeks did this, but they would rub fur over a decent-sized bead of amber and watch as the little hairs would reach out and cling to the amber like a child to their mother. They did not know what this was about or what secret of the universe they were dancing around, but they knew something was there. Later, Benjamin Franklin and William Faraday would recreate the experiment without notes from the other. While we all know Benjamin Franklin and his experiment with electricity (don't try it, there are people killed each year attempting it without all Ben's precautions), not everyone knows Faraday.

William Faraday would go on to be named the Father of Electronics. If you've ever heard of a Faraday cage, it's from him. A Faraday cage protects electronics from an electromagnetic pulse. You have one in your home. If you're worried about an EMP destroying all your electronics, put them in a washing machine. Preferably, use a dry machine and don't turn it on (also unplug it).

When describing this static electricity in 1600, William Gilbert called it electricity to hearken back to the ancient Greeks using bits of polished amber or electron. Later, of course, when we discovered that there were particles smaller than atoms (which makes no sense as atom means *indivisible*), we came up with the oxymoronic term subatomic particle. Naming the parts, they found that one particle was responsible for all these electric phenomena and thus named it: electron. Think of it as an ode to history.

Amber, in this case, was a human female, and her big boss needed to get in touch with me. Am I being called on the carpet? I showed up, glistening and ready. Drama? No. Something bad, maybe. The question was asked, "Was it possible?" Could I tell them if on such and such a day if a person used their PIN?

Sit back and watch the magic.

If they could give me the date and either the last four of the card or the dollar amount, I could tell them:

- Card type (MC/Visa, Diner's Club…)

- Whether credit or debit

- Whether the PIN was used or not

- Time of day

- Rewards card or not

- The person's zodiac or sun sign

- …and if they like Chinese food, rainy days, and long walks on the beach

Now, I know what you're thinking. *Diner's Club, Will? Really?* Yeah, man. It still exists. I know, I know, but it's out there. Though Telly is gone, you can almost hear, "Who loves you, baby?" His real name is Aristotelis. He's Greek. No, I'm not on a Greek thing. Discover card bought and still owns Diner's Club, which has a very limited capacity.

As I told them, the point is when it came to that, I was like the world's greatest tracker, Prince Humperdink from *The Princess Bride*. As Buttercup said, "He can track a falcon on a cloudy day! He can find you!" I was like that, except it was not due to some preternatural skill. A transaction was trackable by MC/Visa to the nth degree because its card, type, how it was used, and all its facets decide *how it will be charged*. If that couldn't be tracked, all their billions of dollars are up in the air.

I have seen a transaction fee in the thousands—just the fee. Now, imagine the difference between that fee being rated as 0.89 percent and 3.1 percent. That is a greater than 2 percent range or more than tripled. How many fees would you like to see tripled? How many fees are you okay with them tripling? The answer for me is zero. (ZEE-roh. Noun. Syn: Nada, Goose-egg, zilch.)

As it turns out, a debit card had been used, and there was no PIN (**P**ersonal **I**dentification **N**umber) entered, so no PIN-based debit. That was an issue. Apparently, an overzealous person took a card, something went South, the margin was already thin, and problems ensued. I could get them all they needed and more, but it was reporting the news they didn't want. At least they now knew what happened in explicit detail.

They also knew I could always get the data if need be.

18

WHAT A BANK DOESN'T DO AND NEITHER DID EDISON

Do you know? Sure, they don't make spaghetti or Ferris wheels. True. That's all true, but they don't set up merchant accounts, either. Really. They want you to think they do.

While I am blowing minds here, understand that Edison did *not* invent the lightbulb. I know, I know. Go ahead and Google it. The rest of us will wait here. Done? See, what he did not do was invent the light bulb. However, he spent the rest of his natural-born life encouraging people to think he did. I'm not kidding.

How did he get away with that? The stinker! In all fairness, Edison is the reason we have the light bulb. You repeatedly hear that he tried and failed to make it 1,800 times and would correct people and say that he never failed; he just found 1,799 ways or so *not* to make a bulb, which is also important. Sometimes, when building, you have to learn what doesn't work.

The true story is that he tried 1,800 or so times to make a (pay attention here) light bulb *filament* that was inexpensive. One can make just about anything, but it must be affordable to market it. Make one first, then see where you can make it cheaply. He ended up using bamboo fibers with carbon deposited on them. *Voila!*

Banks are not unlike this story. They just don't really do merchant accounts. They want you to think that they do, but they do not. *No*, just like the old Arby's fast-food commercial, where a person would have a virtual Arby's hat floating over their head as they said the tagline, "I'm thinking Arby's," banks know that they have a virtual dollar symbol that floats over them.

Think about it. Maybe not on all banks, but at least when you drive past your bank, you think of *money*. Whether you see coins, paper, plastic, checks, or gold bullion, you think it. And as we think emotionally and in pictures, we see something. That something is how we think of money.

This is the first trap. Know of its existence.

Knowing lets you understand the situation, and understanding makes you safer. I always tell clients who feel baffled because they called in to speak to their processor and got intimidated right off the phone: Don't call them. Their job is to get you off the phone. Call your specialist. A specialist cannot be confused or intimidated. They will not be tricked by an MC/Visa "officer." They know those sign-up fees are bogus and that machines are all but, and sometimes are, free. They can't be surprised by arcane jargon. They cut right through that because *use makes mastery*, and they use it daily.

Most importantly, I said to call *your* specialist. Man or woman, they work for you. They should be purely performance based. Your best interest is their best interest. A good specialist won't put you in a situation that is good for them and bad for you. Besides being bad for you, it would eventually blow up and damage your reputation. An older woman vouching for me because I chased her to give back $2 did not seem like a big deal then. I have come to appreciate my actions better since then. We all must say, "Good for my client is good for me." Only that and nothing more.

When I have a client who calls—be it a company that makes $5,000 a month in total sales or a company that does millions every month without effort—and asks for something, I have but one response, "I work for you." I say it loud and often, and I let everyone from the firm's partners to the newest staff members hear me say it. I work for you. They all hear it. It's practically a company motto. If I say it, then they had sure-as-you're-born better say it. That's because, after all these years, my grandmother was right: You work for too long and too hard to get a customer in the door to lose one. She meant because you didn't take their kind of payment. Amen to that. Also, your clients are your lifeblood. Treat them well. Treat them as you would your grandmother if she had an account with your business.

It's hard to go wrong with that mentality.

Your training ends with some ideas from Victor Hugo's masterwork *Les Misérables*. Victor Hugo died and was buried in France with every award the French nation could give a non-military citizen. His pen was his sword, and he could craft such works that are hard to describe without his powers. When you can laugh, weep, and want to throw a book down in one and a half chapters, you know he had firmly reached through his pen via those pages and grabbed you by the heart.

He was an excellent scholar in his own right. For him to go off on a tangent for fifty pages was nothing. After he wrote about the French sewer system for eighty pages, I could have told you everything about it. Architecture not your thing? Fine, how about military history? After over fifty pages on the Battle of Waterloo, I could have taken a final exam for a terminal-level degree in military history and aced it. It would just go on and on, yet you were never lost.

The Thenardiers in his book were the lowest form of life. They were merciless and mercenary in their dealings. They ran a hotel where they would scrape you free of every penny you might barely have. In the musical, they do a great job of this in lyrical form.

"Charge 'em for the mice,
Extra for the lice,
Two percent for looking in the mirror twice…"

It is sad to say that this is a good example of what to think of your bank and its providers. They are not the March of Dimes. They are there to charge you. Granted, it's for a service or product, but they will charge you. I have said this earlier, and I will repeat it. Everyone up the food chain makes money off your merchant account. If your rate goes up, they all make more. The only person who makes less is *you*.

This is the second trap. Know of its existence.

The Thenardiers were a terrible and ruthless family. They bled people dry, risked the lives and health of their own children, and were willing to run any scheme or con for nothing more than a little bit of money. As time passed, there was nothing they would not do. All was on the table.

Is your bank that bad? No, of course not. We have a different kind of issue in the world today: the blind, faceless corporation. This is a behemoth (and I use that word very much on purpose) that is a giant, slow-moving Hulk. Fighting it is like fighting a fog. There is almost nothing to actually fight. Did somebody purposefully, with malice and intent, do something to you, your business, or your account? No. But nothing was done to prevent something from happening either, save fraud.

They build massive pieces to fight against, track, and prevent fraud. This is for two key purposes. The first is simply to cover their backsides. Yes, that's true. I'm sorry. Everything in the system isn't to protect you. In fact, as a business, you get thrown under the bus first. No, it's to protect them, and by "them," I mean the system, namely from lawsuits. If certain key pieces and elements are put in place, didn't they do what they could to protect them? Sure. Also, you indemnify them heavily and often. Everything you do protects and indemnifies them.

The second is to protect the cardholder, which means the system. If you believe in the system and that it works, you will go out, use your plastic, and buy stuff.

This is hard to overstate.

The concept of relying on something and trusting in it is what society is built on. Think of the roadways. This, next to spoken language, is one of the single most pivotal parts of the world. Knowing that we can use and trust our system speeds up everything we do. It allows us to travel, which, like speech, allows everything else. We trust that the roads and their maintenance—the signs, the lights, and, most importantly, that everyone else will use them (within reason) accordingly. Because we have that trust in the system, we can use it without thinking much about it. That means we rely on it and use it more heavily than ever. Imagine how slow everything would be if we drove around like an alien from another world, unsure how the roadways would run and how safe we would be on them.

The system—in terms of businesses and their acceptance of cards—is pivotal to the movement and growth of a nation. The individual user, all the millions of them, must act almost like a hive and trust that the queen and all the other bees know what the heck they're doing. If you were unsure if your card would work every time you went to swipe it, you'd swipe it a lot less.

19

THE STRENGTH OF SAMPSON

People often make a mistake in the tale of Sampson, thinking that Sampson's strength was in his hair, which had never been cut—not at all. I mean, yes, that was an issue, but it was the straw that broke the camel's back.

Sampson was to be what was called a Nazarite—not a Nazarene (someone from Nazareth), mind you. This was a special thing; a vow and a special title were put upon a person, and strict things went along with it. Not that this is odd, as we have such things even today, just like the men who work as guards at the Tomb of the Unknown Soldier. These men must be of the highest caliber. They train. They know their routines cold. They are formally known as Sentinels, and they guard the tomb in the strictest formality twenty-four hours a day, 365 days a year, in heat, rain, sleet, and snow. They do not drink on or off duty—ever. They take an oath that they will not drink for the rest of their natural lives.

Why such focus and determination? Think about it. These Sentinels guard the tomb of a man who made the ultimate sacrifice for his country, its values, and its beliefs. He didn't merely die for his nation; he could not even be identified and sent home to rest. His family never saw his return, either with his shield or on it. It's an extra blow, even for the dead, and yet it makes him every man on the battlefield. It makes him any soldier, and thus *the* soldier.

For this reason—because he fought and died and carries such a symbol—the men who guard him guard a bit of America's heart. Its undefinable courage is expressed in this tomb. The tomb is not the flag but around the flag, about the flag, and, yes, buried under the flag.

These men and women don't drink because they may do or say something that would taint their duty and, by association, the tomb. Think of that kind of commitment. Think of that level of service.

A Nazarite was a religious elite and was to follow certain things to keep him ceremonially clean, so he was set apart from the rest. This is not odd, as the word sanctified meant "to be set apart." To be a Nazarite, you had to follow three rules.

1. Touch no dead thing.

2. Drink no strong drink.

3. Do not cut one's hair.

Stick with me for just a moment as I unpack this tale.

In the Bible, only two examples of Nazarites are ever noted. Historians and theologians know there were more, but only these two are mentioned: Sampson and his mother. We never learn her name as all she is referred to as is Manoah's wife. We do know that she was effectively sterile, and this was a great source of pain to her. She wanted a child and finally had a divine message telling her she would bear a son. Here's the thing: He must be a Nazarite from birth. Most Nazarites choose to become so. Think of a scout wanting to get to be an Eagle Scout. This was not Sampson. He was to be one from birth, which meant his mother must take the Nazarite vow and *not* do the three things on the Nazarite Naughty List. So, as we can see, Manoah's wife is a Nazarite, only to make Sampson a Nazarite from birth. In effect, even from conception and, thus, forever.

But he breaks the rules. His temper, wanting things now, and vanity lead to a great fall. But it is not the hair. At least it's not *just* the hair. Because you see, he broke all three rules. He drank. He touched a dead lion—the lion he killed with his bare hands when he came back upon it and saw the bees had made a hive. Sampson was big, and he broke into the honeycomb hideout built in a dead animal's carrion to satisfy a sweet tooth. Two down. One to go.

Finally, *finally,* he gave in to Delilah. He should have known. Several times, she asked the source of his strength. Whatever he told her, she did, and she called in enemy warriors that Sampson defeated—every time. In case you're confused, I mean every time she enacted exactly what he said was his weakness and called in enemy warriors, *and* every time, he defeated them. Do you know the old saying, "Fool me once, shame on you; fool me twice, shame on me"? This was three of four times she asked, he told her, and she did exactly what he said would defeat him. Then, he finally got to his true kryptonite. He told her, and she cut it. I remember my Bible teacher in fourth grade telling me exactly this. That Sampson loved Delilah, but it never said Delilah loved Sampson. She cut his hair and called in the enemy, and he was beaten.

Even Sampson got it wrong. What he should have said was that he had drunk a strong drink and touched a dead thing, and all that was left was his hair that had never been cut. When she cut his hair, it was the final straw. All three were broken. He lost the strength that led to his great vanity.

I write this because I have never seen a business with one issue. They always have multiple, and they are sucking the very strength out of the business. The last non-profit I worked with at the time of this writing had its three maladies. Two you have heard before. They could not read their statements. This blindness kept them from seeing the bloodletting. They had massive creep, made worse because they simply could not see it. The third blow was the PCI fee eating away at them month after month.

20

PCI FEES AND THE ATTACK SINISTER

B ad news is bad news. This will sound mercenary, but it's good for me. If everything was honkey-dory, I'd have no work. All my sales would be based solely on my pretty face. Don't get me wrong; I am strikingly good looking. As I walk by, flowers turn away from the sun to face me. Yeah, they sure do.

Creep is bad enough. Death by a thousand pinpricks will bleed a company dry over time. A lack of understanding is also disastrous. If you can't read your P&L, how do you know if you are doing well or about to close? If you can't read your statement for your merchant account, you might as well be a stranger in a strange land and hope that people will always do their best for you. But the PCI is a small secret knife aimed at the heart of your business.

I learned to fence in college. It was an exciting sport—fast and vicious—but it required untold finesse and control. If you think you can walk into a fencing salle (the area where one trains) and swing a foil, saber, or epee like Conan the Cimmerian, you will have your backside handed to you on a French platter. The history of fencing is an evolution, as it is with all things. We see a lot of attacks and parries in sword fight movie scenes. A parry is a sword used to block an attack.

I got to send them a statement showing they would save $21,000 a year. Great. No kidding. Hasn't that always been the case? No. Blocking with a blade comes late in the game. They used everything and every technique. You could dodge the opponent's blade. You could slap it away with a cloak or cape. You could grab it with your left hand if you had a special mailed glove of metal rings protecting you from being cut. You could even use a shield or usually a buckler. A buckler is a small shield, a little smaller than a dinner plate. Young men studying the art of fencing used to have a sword, a knife, and a buckler dangling from their hips as they walked about bar hopping in the night, looking for wine, women, and revelry. The buckler would dangle and bang about as it swashed to and fro, giving them a little bling back in the day. Where do you think the term "swashbuckler" comes from, anyway?

The left-handed knife became very popular. The French called it the *main gauche* or left hand. Frank Herbert, in his book *Dune,* called it something else. In a science fantasy world that lived in a feudal system with lasers and everything else, he brought back the sword in combat due to a science fiction invention of his simply called the shield. A shield was a force field worn on the body. Nothing fast-moving made it through. People were trained at a young age to fence with swords and knives and move fast enough to maneuver around their opponent and slow enough to penetrate the shield. Fast-moving things were deflected. The slow blade penetrated the shield.

They would fence with a sword with a longer blade and a knife in their left hand. He called it "the attack sinister." Sinister is anything in terms of the left hand. In coats of arms, the heraldic devices on the left are sinister. Of course, this has a double meaning for Herbert and history.

Things from the right hand were good, and from the left were bad. Don't shoot the messenger if you're a southpaw. My eldest sister is as well. That's just the way things were. Herbert meant this as a sneaky little backup. After all, if the sword is an extension of the arm and an enemy gets inside the sword's reach, it's very hard to get back far enough to keep them on the pointy side of your weapon.

But you could still attack if you had a knife, a smaller blade in your left hand that was more agile than a sword. This sneaky little reserve piece was his attack sinister. It was left-handed, supposedly secret, and maybe a little dastardly.

I loved fencing and the book *Dune*. I do not like the PCI compliance fee. It is designed to help defray the cost of policing everything and keeping it safe. You pay it to protect the customer and, ultimately, the system. It also is a money maker. Like that one subscription that you signed up for a trial and immediately forgot about (and didn't proactively go in and turn it off), it started billing you monthly, automatically. Bleed, bleed, bleed. Here's the difference. You never had a choice but to sign up for this club. If you get a merchant account, you have a PCI fee. No one is grandfathered into their old system, so they don't have to pay for it. It was slapped on everyone.

And it goes up.

Yes, up. Don't worry. You do not have to think about it, really. They'll just take it out every month. You do have to renew it every year, and by renew, I mean check in on or before the birthday of your account, fill out a technical survey, double-check what you're doing, and send it in. It kind of sounds like renewing your car tag, doesn't it? The difference is an expired car tag might get you a ticket. A PCI non-compliance fee is charged every month, month after month. It's easy for this once $5 to $15 monthly fee to jump to $35 or even $99 monthly. However, I have seen non-compliance fees north of $100 monthly. This last one was

$123 a month—month after month (after month), perpetual like Netflix. If you don't have your calculator handy, that's $1,476 a year. But never fear, it will charge you again on the thirteenth month. It won't end after just one year. Attack sinister, indeed.

Do they reach out to you? Yes. Do they let you know you have to do this? Yes. Do I think, after my years in the industry, that this is *absolutely* set up in such a way with lots of psychology involved to help you and improve the odds you won't do it because, dang, you are busy? Yes, oh yes.

Now, add that almost $1,500 bill to the other over-spending that happens because your rate is creeping up, and you can't read your statement. All three rules are broken. Sampson fell—even the great Sampson himself.

IV

It's the End

1

FEAR AND LOATHING...

It's easy to read through the described pain here and get an overwhelming sense of dread. It looks and sounds very much like it is bad and can only go bad. I get that.

It's not. Like anything, if you watch it, you manage it. If you do it regularly, you master it. The industry preys on people not wanting to watch it. They designed it not to be followed vigorously. A little training and having a specialist in the field go a long way. Learn the basics and know the traps. Then, you will be much further along than most.

"The first step in avoiding a trap is *knowing* of its existence," stated Thufir Hawat, Master of Assassins. He didn't train assassins. That was not his mastery. No, he trained people how to avoid assassins and not be caught by them. He was a master of all their tricks and trained people to *survive*. You know of these traps now. Go and be safe.

If you need help with anything here, or would just like someone to do the math for you, go to https://qr.link/dMiltp or click the QR code and we'll take it from there.

About the Author

Will Black has spent the last twenty-four years in the payments industry. He started in the bullpen in a card payment software company, earned his corner office and leather chair in eighteen months, then hung his own shingle. His firm also designed credit card processing software, and he sold the company and started his own merchant firm.

Then came the pivotal day when he met a symphony that had closed due to infighting and bad budgets. When they tried to relaunch, no one would even take their calls. That's when Will stepped in and explained how the payments industry worked and how the "built-in" fee had a percentage that went back to the banking system but could go to charity. It was a hit, and he redirected $50,000 to this charity.

Since then, he has helped businesses automate their philanthropy and give millions to charities that would have usually just gone back into the system. He lives in Savannah, GA, with his beautiful red-headed wife, two children, and a Boston Terrier in a house with many sea life and ship decorations.